Ruth:
The Story is in the Names

Sally Meredith

ISBN: 1490559884
ISBN 13: 9781490559889
Library of Congress Control Number: 2014904169
CreateSpace Independent Publishing Platform
North Charleston, South Carolina

Sally Meredith's well-crafted stories and scriptural guidance are fresh and relevant, and lead us to seek answers to problems where we struggle. She relays the unmistakable message of God's ability to meet our every need—despite our circumstances. Ruth lived in uncertain times but discovered how faith in God made a big difference. Centuries have passed but times have not changed. Be prepared to be blessed.

Maxine Marsolini
Speaker, radio program and author of *Blended Families, Raising Children in Blended Families, Blended Families Workbook, and Rebuilding Families One Dollar At A Time.*

Did you know your circumstances matter to God? That your trials, your work, and even your legacy matters to God? "Ruth, The story is in the Names," will teach you about the book of "Ruth," but also about your life. Your life matters to God! I highly recommend this wonderful and insightful book!

Linda Dillow Speaker, author of: *Creative Counterpart; Calm My Anxious Heart; Satisfy My Thirsty Soul,* and more

Sally's study is diligently researched, compellingly thought-provoking and consistently encouraging. Though Ruth is the star, it is Naomi, a woman whose sufferings rival Job's, who is the backbone and inspiration of the story. From the position of mother-in-law, with sorrow and often flagging faith, she forges forth with dogged determination. Her life produces lasting fruit for eternity. This book inspires us that through our own sufferings God can bring forth fruit for His Kingdom.

Robert Andrews and wife Jill
Founder of Gospel Parenting, coach, teaching elder
Author of *The Family, God's Weapon for Victory, The Scandalous Gospel of God's Grace, A Glorious Church,* and more.

A lot of people who write, in my opinion, don't have moral authority because what is in the head has never gotten to the heart. The joy of knowing Sally for over 40 years is that her heart lives out God's Word. She has been a passionate follower of Jesus Christ. Sally goes deep with these two women, Naomi and Ruth, who have much to teach us about the love of our Savior, and the joy of submission to His Lordship and leadership. Her insights are very practical and uplifting for all of us who desire to follow Jesus.

John Maisel

Past President of Eastern European Seminary, Founder and Chairman Emeritus of East-West Ministries, Intl., author of: *Surprised by Grace*

I have been enjoying a Ruth/Naomi type of mentoring relationship with Sally for many years! Her joy in the Lord and gift for teaching His Word, give the pages of this book life and breath. They bring hope to any who cannot see the hand of the Lord in their present circumstances but hold unswervingly to the hope that He is. Sally's exploration of the suffering and faith of Ruth and Naomi show the reader that God truly works all things together for good.

Melissa Gibbs, Wife of J.D. Gibbs, President of Joe Gibbs Racing, Inc.

Sally Meredith's faith and storytelling enthusiasm are evident in her re-creation of Ruth. Sally vividly describes God's painting that brings light into a dark world. She vulnerably shares the trials that she and her family have endured. Their witness is a path of faith, inspiring others, including us. Her book speaks to the unending and unfailing love of a God who is sovereign over all.

Ed Bethune and wife Lana

Former Arkansas Congressman, author of *Gay Panic in the Ozarks, Jackhammered: A Congressman's Memoir, Blue Water Sailing and Believing*

My friend and colleague in ministry, Sally Meredith, has had a long and effective ministry in winning others to Christ and teaching them the faith. She has drawn on this experience, and her own as a wife and mother, in writing a warm, personal reflection on the Book of Ruth with an eye to its applications for women in particular. Her thoughtful recounting of the relationship, trials and triumphs of Ruth and Naomi will touch hearts and encourage faith.

Rev. Timothy Crater and wife Sherry
Pastor, co-author of *In God We Trust: Stories of Faith in American History,* writer for *Community Bible Study*

RUTH conveys the love of Yahweh and how His sovereign plan, sometimes through pain and suffering, brings depth, meaning and hope to the lives of those who follow Him. The richness of the relationship between Naomi and Ruth offers purpose to each us as we are His ministers of reconciliation. Naomi's reflection of the love of Yahweh caused Ruth to say "Your people will be my people and your God will be my God". Sally Meredith and husband Don have impacted untold tens of thousands of lives in like manner as Naomi. We have been blessed to have been recipients of their deep love and encouragement for 40 years.

Rep. Robert Pittenger and wife Suzanne, N.C. Congress

Sally Meredith is a lifelong learner. She is able to take the Word of God and the truths that God reveals to her and pass them on in such a way that people can understand and apply to their lives. She is a wonderful teacher, highly qualified, and a seeker of truth. She makes "Ruth" come alive.

Dr. Barry Leventhal and wife Mary
Distinguished Senior Professor, Former Provost and Academic Dean, Southern Evangelical Seminary, publications for *Christian Apologetics Journal, Theological Perspectives on the Holocaust, A Biblical Theology of Israel and the Jews.*

Drawing on her years of Bible study, mentoring, and teaching, Sally explores the experience of faith in the face of grief and the often delicate mother-in-law and daughter-in-law relationship. Her insights and reflections on hope, love, loss and God's redemption will inspire and empower you.

Ann Conway, speaker, teacher

The book of Ruth comes from the Old Testament. The story I have laid out will become clear as we contemplate the names in the story and what they mean. The story unfolds as the names unfold, ending with the last name, which defines our ultimate Redeemer, Jesus Christ. God weaves His own names throughout the story, showing His characteristics of a caring and loving Heavenly Father. This is a timeless story of love, redemption, tragedy and joy. The circumstances could be events of any era, any age, within any family.

Dedication:

To my widowed friends
and friends who've lost a child,
you have suffered much.
Your strength and faith
are an ever present testimony
to those of us who watch.

And to my very special daughter-in-law,
Sara Bergman Meredith
Thank you for loving my son.

Contents

Acknowledgments

Writing a book in my old age has proven to be a more difficult task than I surmised. While still in embryo form several women gladly took "their women" through the manuscript and gave invaluable input. Dixie Fraley Keller, Lisa Powell, and Ann Conway, you are loved.

Special thanks to my group of women who met weekly to give advise and rearrange content: Ann Conway, Marilyn Nutter, Tiffany Haines, Rebecca Mullet, Meg Henry, Margaret McKinney, Tammy Martinez. Tim and Sherry Crater gave theological input and suggestions to the manuscript.

Thanks to internet friends who have given their time and talent to further this project: Brenda Lawrence, Caroline Finley, Mary Leventhal, Lorianne Merritt, John Maisel, Sharyn Regier, Jill Andrews, Carol Sarian, Maxine Marsolini, Melissa Gibbs, Lana Bethune. I could not have done this without you, my dear friends.

Thanks to my editor, Tim Grissom. I will be forever in your debt.

Thanks also to Amazon CreateSpace team. Thank you for your help and expertise.

A special thank you to my wonderful children and their spouses who constantly show me in more ways than you know that God has arms of love manifested in your lives. Thank you for producing for me those amazing gifts of grandchildren. My quiver is rejoicing.

And last, to my husband of 47 years–thank you for your undying faith love for me and for always believing in me and having my back. You have encouraged me in more ways than you will ever know. I'll love you for always.

Introduction

The Connection of Story

As a young adult, reading books was not my highest priority. However, something clicked for me in my mid-thirties when I was challenged to read biographies of famous missionaries and Christian leaders. I found that these stories grabbed my attention and literally gave me a track to run on in times of trial and discouragement. These true-to-life stories of risky faith in harsh realities motivated me in my spiritual journey.

During that same period I dusted off my Bible and discovered the ancient text of the Old Testament. Having been raised in church, I knew some of the children's Bible stories like Adam and Eve, Jonah and the whale, and Daniel in the lion's den. But I saw them as disconnected stories with different meanings. Then I began to recognize that history was connected through story, each story built upon the one before it. Understanding biblical history had been like trying to put the pieces of a puzzle together without seeing the top of the box; it was confusing at best. When I discovered that a specific genealogy *was* the top of the box, everything began to fall into proper place and make sense. That genealogy was the line of the Messiah running from Adam to Jesus Christ.

By reading the stories in the Old Testament, history began to be enjoyable to me. But it took some time to study and decipher. I had many "ah ha" moments as I began to unravel the mysteries of life found in the varied adventures of God's kingdom builders. God has been on the march throughout history to find people whose hearts are fully His. In telling His story the red ribbon of Messianic genealogy connects those stories and makes them come alive and give greater meaning to the whole. The book of Ruth is one of those stories that fits into the larger puzzle.

The Bible is a compilation of stories of people in every walk of life: from kings to paupers, from the spiritual to the non-spiritual, from judges to the judged, from the young to the old. The Bible never sugarcoats life, but is brutally honest when it comes to the shortcomings of men and women contrasted with the awesome grace and mercy of God.

God is a God of adventure and romance. He is the author of intrigue, twists and turns, and ultimately the author of "and they lived happily ever after." All good tales take on the essence of the gospel story: the king's son seeks a bride among the ordinary, or he disguises himself in order to win his bride. All "feel good" movies teach that good wins over evil. Within every quality story we find good and evil, tragedy and triumph. And the stories that become our favorites are those that never seem to lose their appeal, no matter what generation reads them. That's why the classics are so . . . classic.

We have before us just such a story. The biblical book of Ruth is a classic from every angle. We find heartache at the deepest level. Adventure abounds. Suspense is woven into the fabric of ordinary lives. God lets us peek through the keyhole at a family living in a perilous time. It's a time of economic uncertainty and fear. The book of Ruth tells the story of God's love and care for the fledgling human race whose only hope is God Himself. In the end, love wins the day.

Isn't that what the Bible is all about? Once all was well and good (Genesis 1-2). Then something happened (Genesis 3) that spoiled everything. The rest of Scripture leads to the last two chapters of Revelation where it will all be made perfect again. We long for that day. We write songs about it. Our hearts are restless until we come to that final rest where all tears are wiped away, and all stories make sense. That's the story of the Bible, the story of the gospel. That's the heart of Ruth's story.

⌒

Mother-in-Law/Daughter-in-Law

Numerous threads are woven into the fabric of the story that is told about Ruth. Relationships are only one thread of the many that make up this particular tapestry. Here we find an unusual bond between a mother-in-law and her daughter-in-law, a rare story indeed. It would not have been unusual to contemplate a story about a mother and her daughter, for that is one of the closest relationships on earth. The bond is so strong that it can sometimes come between the daughter and her spouse. It has been said, "A daughter is a daughter for the rest of her life, but a son is a son until he takes a wife." How true, even today.

I am the mother of three daughters and one son; therefore, I am also a mother-in-law. I met my daughter-in-law, Sara, a number of years ago as she began to date my son. I learned early on that I had to win the trust of someone who had not grown up in my home. A sweet relationship has ensued between Sara and me that I love and am very thankful for, but it took time for both of us. That is not unusual. Unlike Ruth and Naomi, neither of us has lost our spouse and so have not been tested like they were.

I have interviewed many women who have daughters-in-law and many women concerning their mothers-in-law. They all admitted that trust had to be earned. It takes time, many years in fact, to feel comfortable and vulnerable with one another. Managing expectations is a huge factor. Often, there are early disappointments that take time to heal or to reassess. Insights and counsel from others help in the journey. (I have also observed that it is not so different with men and their relationships with fathers-in-law.) In-laws play a major role in the maturation process of life.

For some women, this mother-in-law–daughter-in-law relationship can be one of caring, simply because each one is part of the same family. But for many, this relationship never reaches the level of the comfort longed for. Lack of proximity, differing personalities, and other factors make this a difficult relationship. In my opinion, few succeed to the level of Ruth with Naomi, main characters in the book of Ruth.

Within four short chapters there is a great deal of what I call "white space" in this rendering of the love between this mother-in-law and daughter-in-law. For instance, the first five verses cover the events of ten years. If you think about your last ten years, I'm sure that five short sentences would be inadequate to tell your story. When Scripture says something clearly, I take it for what it says. When Scripture is silent, I believe God allows some latitude and contemplation about what may have happened.

Most commentaries on the book of Ruth seem to conjecture on some issues. A good friend and theologian, Dr. Barry Leventhal, gave me this advice: "What does it say? If it doesn't say, then you have the freedom to develop a theory based on other verses that may have a bearing on the theory." My theories vary from many that I have read. While I don't presume to know all the answers, as I read the text and contemplated the white spaces, I have based my thoughts on other verses in the book as well as other passages of Scripture. These theories will become clear as we progress.

Running The Race In Faith

Between the pages of history the Bible highlights people who learned to walk by faith in an unseen God. These are people who experienced tough lives. Hebrews 11 lists how people of the Old Testament lived by faith in a darkened world. This chapter sets forth a race that we as believers are running. It's a relay race. While the people we meet in the book of Ruth are not listed in "The Hall of Faith" in Hebrews 11, they certainly are a part of the "cloud of witnesses" of Hebrews 12 because these are unnamed people, both past and present. They lived and died in extraordinary faith, and urge us on in our own life. Hear what God has to say about those who have gone before us and how they lived a life of faith.

"through faith, though Abel is dead, he still speaks" (v. 4)

"And without faith it is impossible to please *Him*, for he who comes to God must believe that He is and *that* He is a rewarder of those who seek Him." (v. 6)

"And all these, having gained approval through their faith, did *not* receive what was promised, because God had provided something better for us, so that apart from us they would not be made perfect." (v. 39)

In a relay race there are four runners. The race isn't over until the last person finishes. Then the rewards are given to the team who wins. Just so in the Christian life. Millions of people have already run their leg of the race. The baton is passed from generation to generation. It's not over until all have finished. The final lap, no one knows except God Himself. He knows when the last person who will ever run accepts Him as Savior and begins his race. Until that day, we who are alive are running the race set before us. The baton has been passed to us. It's our time to run.

> Therefore, since we have so great a cloud of witnesses surrounding us, let us also lay aside every encumbrance and the sin which so easily entangles us, and let us run with endurance the race that is set before us, fixing our eyes on Jesus, the author and perfecter of faith, who for the joy set before Him endured the cross, despising the shame, and has sat down at the right hand of the throne of God. (Hebrews 12:1-2)

Every believer, past and present, is admonished by God to keep our eyes on Him and not to look around at our culture for direction. Most directions will come from Scripture. Other directions will come from godly people who have the maturity to help us in this race we are running.

The cloud of witnesses is not only made up of those people who have run and died (they still speak), but also of people who are alive and encouraging us in our race. We are admonished to study the lives of God's people and not be ignorant of what God is teaching us through them. Not only men and women in Scripture, but missionaries and believers' biographies in our day help give encouragement to us. Every believer's story contributes to our own. We learn faith from studying their lives. It's as though they step from the sidelines to give cups of cold water to parched souls. They tell their story and it helps us run our race without grumbling and complaining.

The book of Ruth highlights women of faith who are part of the cloud of witnesses. Naomi and Ruth encourage me as a woman to keep running the race set before me. One day I too will cross the finish line and be numbered with those generations before me.

When we want to remember heroes we put their names on a wall. Will there be such a wall in heaven with our heroes of the faith written there? Will your name and mine be etched on that wall? Will our fingers run over names such as Elimelech, Naomi, Ruth, and Boaz? At the end of the wall will they be standing there ready to welcome us? Will Jesus say to us, "Come, good and faithful servant. You have much to learn and many stories to hear." I can't wait.

Chapter 1

Your Backstory Matters to God

And without faith it is impossible to please Him, for he who comes to God must believe that He is and that He is a rewarder of those who seek Him.

—Hebrews 11:6

All stories have a backstory: a set of circumstances and events that lead up to the main storyline. For instance, my personal backstory includes the Great Depression, even though I was born just after it in 1940. My parents lived through it, eventually marrying during one of the bleakest economic times in American history, and what they experienced greatly influenced how I was brought up and what my values became.

My parents had almost no worldly goods. They were, in the words of the old idiom, "poor as church mice." They paid cash for everything, and would save for months or even years before making large purchases. When we bought a car, Dad would keep it for ten years, fixing every rattle and dent himself. We lived without indoor plumbing until Dad could afford to install it on his own.

Their values became mine: work hard and don't incur debt. Although these values have been tough at times, overall they have served me well. I married a man with these same values, so conflicts have been rare in this area of our marriage.

Another value I learned has to do with fairness in dealing with people. My mother was overly conscious about fairness in raising my sister and me. Decisions, actions, and purchases were carried out with that ideal in mind. I never felt my parents were partial to either of us. Consequently, I too have a strong sense of justice and fairness. Now, I must admit that this has made me a little cross from time to time when things don't seem to be fair, even though God never promised that life would be fair.

I became a Christian at a church camp when I was nine. God's love for me recorded in His Word still amazes me after decades of living life surrounded by unbelief in our society. My faith in God prepared me for the career I would have, for who I would marry and how I would raise my own children. My faith has never waivered, no matter how difficult the circumstances of life.

As a child, I also learned the value of adapting to new situations. I grew up in the mountains of Colorado just outside Boulder and rode a bus to school every day. Because we were rural children, we were placed at different schools each year, depending on availability of space. I attended seven different schools even though our family hadn't moved. Talk about trying to make new friends every year! My sister and many of my friends hated the change, but I actually enjoyed the variety and making new friends.

This served me well later in life when I married Don, because we moved often in ministry. We served with Campus Crusade for Christ in several different states. After leaving Crusade, we started Christian Family Life, and then FamilyLife, (a subsidiary of Crusade headed by Dennis Rainey). Don and I were also church planters in various cities (eight churches in all). Friendships formed quickly and easily for me as we lived in seven different states and fourteen different houses. My childhood background had prepared me for our many moves and transitions.

In addition to the values I carried from childhood to adulthood, I have learned two lessons by connecting my backstory to my story: (1) God is the author of the larger story in which all our individual stories exist, and only within His story do we find purpose and direction for our own. (2) While we are the lead character in our own story, we play supporting roles in the stories of others. We interact with them as they encounter trials, and we find encouragement in our own dramas. The stories of others, past and present, good and bad, help us find our way through the maze of life, and encourage us to run persistently in our own race.

The Backstory of Ruth: A History Lesson

Much like the history-shaping era of the Great Depression helped form me as an adult, so the background of the nation of Israel played a huge part in the story of the biblical account of Ruth. The placement of Ruth, (following Judges in the Bible) is often a mistaken timeline. Ruth doesn't follow but takes place *within* the much larger setting of the Judges. What precedes her and what follows her time is as important as it would be in any story. It helps us understand how she fits into the larger story of God's kingdom-building strategy.

Elimelech and Naomi were born in the early years of Israel's land history. Prior to this time, the children of Israel were nomadic, even though some 430 years previously, God had promised the land of Canaan to Abraham and his descendants (Genesis 15:13; Exodus 12:40). Until that promise was fulfilled, the Israelites were homeless wanderers. They settled in Egypt for a few hundred years, where they were forced into slavery.

The Israelites had come out of Egypt under the strong leadership of Moses. The distance from Egypt to Canaan was relatively short, but the journey took forty years. Why? Because the people griped and grumbled about even the smallest of things. They fought, argued, and rebelled. They grew weary and wanted to go back to Egypt, blaming God and the leader He had appointed for their every hardship. They forsook God and worshipped a golden calf. Their minds were so enslaved by the circumstances of their past experience, horrible though they were, that the people were unable to fully follow God. As a result God let every person of that generation die in the wilderness, except for two faithful men: Joshua and Caleb.

The survivors, all age forty and younger, had never been slaves in Egypt. Their parents and grandparents had been slaves, but not them. It was General Joshua who took the leadership reins from Moses and under his command this huge army of Israelite men conquered the land and their families settled.

The conquest of Canaan and the division of the land into twelve sections (one for each tribe) took a number of years. This was a turbulent time in the life of this new nation – a nation forged on the anvil of bloodshed. As is the case with all humanity, wars settled the land, peace ensued and families began to multiply. Most countries of the world at that time were settled by tribes who often fought and stole from one another, especially over grain. During and after

Gideon's judgeship (Judges 6), landowners would sleep beside their crops until they were brought to market. This occurred in the book of Ruth.

In the beginning of these land settlements, judges were appointed to set boundaries and settle disputes (like our governors). Now, you would think that with all their training in obedience during the wilderness wandering the people would have maintained a strong devotion to God as they settled in the land He had given them. But people are fallen. When things went well, they all but forgot God. This led to three hundred years of "the cycles of judges" in which the nation spiritually declined time after time. These cycles—there were seven in all—are described in the Old Testament book of Judges.

The Cycles of Judges

> Then the LORD raised up judges who delivered them from the hands of those who plundered them. Yet they did not listen to their judges, for they played the harlot after other gods and bowed themselves down to them. They turned aside quickly from the way in which their fathers had walked in obeying the commandments of the LORD; they did not do as their fathers. When the LORD raised up judges for them, the LORD was with the judge and delivered them from the hand of their enemies all the days of the judge; for the LORD was moved to pity by their groaning because of those who oppressed and afflicted them. But it came about when the judge died, that they would turn back and act more corruptly than their fathers, in following other gods to serve them and bow down to them; they did not abandon their practices or their stubborn ways. (Judges 2:16–19)

Each cycle began with the people doing whatever they pleased ("what was right in [their] own eyes"), followed by God punishing them by provoking other nations to invade and defeat them. Then, finding themselves in a hopeless situation, the people would beg God for mercy. God would raise up a deliverer—a judge—from among the people who would admonish them to put their trust in God. The people would then trust God for a time, but would sooner or later enter yet another cycle. This went on for three hundred years, from 1350 BC to 1050 BC. They were, as we are so often today, a stiff-necked people, a people called by God, yet they kept forgetting who God was.

All the surrounding nations had kings ruling over them. The people of Israel complained and clamored for a king whom they could see and hear, even though God was to be their King (Judges 17:6; 18:1; 19:1; 21:25).

This is the backstory of Ruth, with the nation in the forgetting-God-and-rebelling part of the cycle. Evil reigned on every street corner, in every field, and in most homes. Men took advantage of women, using them only for selfish pleasure. The government leaders did what they wanted and justified their behavior. Many had more than one wife, or kept numerous concubines and prostitutes as a means of gratifying their sexual appetites.

The book of Judges is full of the evil of mankind. And as that evil spilled over, even those devoted to God suffered the consequences as well.

⌒

Light verses Dark

The book of Ruth was written as a *contrast* to the book of Judges. It's a story of faith in an unbelieving society, obedience among a disobedient people, and hope in an unseen God who orchestrates the paths of those who trust in Him. It demonstrates faith that God would one day provide a Redeemer. The opposite is described in Judges, which reveals a selfish people in desperate need of a redeemer but with no apparent recognition of that fact.

When studying this three-hundred-year period of Israel's history, I see a painting that is very dark. People appear to be aimlessly wandering about with heads bowed in disillusionment. Into that painting, a light, a faint ray of hope begins to appear. It is God's light, dim at first. But as Ruth's story unfolds, the light grows brighter and clearer. This light reveals a family who has a relationship with Him that is the essence of who they are. Why would God highlight them? What about their lives indicates a different perspective of life and motivates them to courageousness?

5

Correlation to History and Today

We may think, *that was then, this is now*, but in many ways we're still living in the time of judges. Looking back on the history of nations, haven't we always done what was right in our own eyes, and haven't we suffered for it? Humanity has generally been godless in every era.

We are doing what is right in our own eyes today. Many say that abortion is a right, others say that sex outside of marriage and among whoever consents is a right. Whatever we want can be framed as a right. We can twist sins, whether personal or national, so they are positioned as rights that take precedence over God's laws and commands.

We should understand, however, that God doesn't give us laws because He wants to make us miserable. God's principles are given because He loves us completely and wants the best for us. He knows that obedience is difficult at times, but it is *best* for us in the long run. He tests us because He knows we are a sinful people wanting to go our own way. We are still His children and He is our Father. Can we trust His heart?

Into every era of history God shines a spotlight on His people, those who follow Him no matter what is happening in their lives or in the culture. The Bible has recorded the life and times of many of these people as examples for us to follow. I believe we have one such before us in the book of Ruth.

God had warned His people what would happen if they forgot who He was and went after their own hearts and lusts.

> Beware lest you forget the LORD your God by not keeping His commandments and His ordinances and His statues which I am commanding you today; otherwise when you have eaten and are satisfied, and have built good houses and lived in them, and when your herds and flocks multiply, and your silver and gold multiply, and all that you have multiplies, then your heart will become proud and you forget the Lord your God . . . Otherwise, you may say in your heart, "My power and the

strength of my hand made me this wealth." . . . It shall come about if you ever forget the LORD your God and go after other gods and serve them and worship them, I testify against you today that you shall surely perish. Like the nations that the LORD makes to perish before you, so you shall perish; because you would not listen to the voice of the LORD your God. (Deuteronomy 8:11–14, 17, 19-20)

Is there a warning here for us? Like other times in history, God wants to bless us as a nation. America has indeed been blessed in the past. Our country was founded upon the same principles of faith in God that Israel was founded upon. But if we, like they, become a nation who forgets God, we will suffer the consequences. Sadly, our own recent history resembles a "cycle of Judges." When our nation suffered the tragic events of 9/11, many turned to God. But this lasted only momentarily. Moral values have since returned to a downward spiral.

Furthermore, many people would not give God the credit for the blessings we experience as a nation in the first place. And when those blessings are taken away, we tend to blame others for our misfortunes instead of seeing God's hand in it. The book of Judges is there to give us warning of the sure consequences of a nation abandoning God. We are not exempt.

We will either be like the people in Judges who disregarded God and followed their own wills, or we will be like the people in Ruth who stand out as lights in the midst of a dark and perverse generation. In *Homan's Old Testament Commentary* (1) a contrast of the times of Judges and Ruth were likened to Charles Dickens quote in his book, *A Tale of Two Cities.* (2)

Ruth	**Judges**
It was the best of times,	it was the worst of times,
it was the age of wisdom,	it was the age of foolishness,
it was the epoch of belief,	it was the epoch of incredulity
it was the season of Light,	it was the season of Darkness,
it was the spring of hope,	it was the winter of despair,
we had everything before us,	we had nothing before us,
we were all going direct to heaven,	we were all going direct the other way.

As we move through this book, ask God to speak to you concerning your relationships with others and with Him. The nuggets of learning we uncover together may be key in your faith journey. Remember, God is building His kingdom through the faith of His people. The characters in the book of Ruth will stand out as ordinary people, going through everyday life, experiencing trials that enhance their faith. This family is part of God's kingdom-building strategy. Is God still on the move today?

Where is our own culture and how can we be a light that shines in a dark world? The picture God is painting is still being completed. He is not finished. You and I are a part of it. Is the darkness stifling to our faith? Are people walking around disillusioned with life? Does our era remind you of the time of the Judges? Will we be people of faith who live in the light or will we add to the darkness? God has always had a people who trust in Him. Let's not buy into the mindset that there's nothing we can do, no matter how dark the painting is around us.

There has never been an era in history, no matter how evil, when the light of God's love was not visible and able to penetrate darkness. It was so during the Middle Ages when Martin Luther opposed the church's ultra-biblical authority and launched a movement that has continued ever since. During the Nazi regime, Aleksandr Solzhenitsyn vocalized his beliefs amid a people blindly following a charismatic yet evil leader named Hitler. In 1948 when Mao Zedong tried to blot out Christianity by forcing missionaries out of China, the church went underground where it has continued to grow into a mighty army. So too, during the great apostasy in Israel from 1350–1050 BC, there arose a family who recognized and proclaimed that God was indeed king over them. They refused to succumb to the popular dissatisfaction of following the unseen God.

Now let's find out about this ordinary family, living within its darkened culture. Would they be light? Or would they be like the people surrounding them?

Chapter Discussion

1. Based on Hebrews 11, describe the importance of personal faith.

   It Changes me, Guides me, transform me

2. Describe your relationship with your mother-in-law or daughter-in-law.

3. In what ways has your backstory contributed to the person you are today?

4. Why are we admonished in Scripture to follow God and obey His principles? When we don't are there consequences?

5. What are some areas where you consider you have "rights"?

6. In a few sentences record the last ten years of your life.

Chapter 2

Your Circumstances Matter to God

In those days there was no king in Israel; everyone did what was right
in his own eyes.

--Judges 21:25

Now it came about in the days when the judges governed, that there was
a famine in the land. And a certain man of Bethlehem in Judah went to
sojourn in the land of Moab with his wife and his two sons. And the name
of the man was Elimelech, and the name of his wife, Naomi; and the names
of his two sons were Mahlon and Chilion, Ephrathites of Bethlehem in
Judah. Now they entered the land of Moab and remained there.

—Ruth 1:1–2

Wanting to be like the surrounding nations, the people of Israel were clamoring for a king. During this very public and widespread dissatisfaction with
God, one couple had a son and named him Elimelech, which means *"our God is
King."* The parents were making a bold statement to their disgruntled countrymen
and leaders. They wanted nothing to do with this movement to change Israel from
the sole leadership of God, a theocracy, to the control of men, a monarchy. People
mistakenly thought a human king could lead them better than the God they couldn't
see, feel, or touch. There were a few, however, who did not think this way. Elimelech's
parents were the kind of people who trusted God, not a man-centered government.

The Importance of Names

We must pause now to contemplate the meaning of names and why they are often overlooked when reading Scripture. In biblical times, names were given for a multitude of reasons.

1) Names told the story of *what was happening in a nation.* Starting with Adam to Noah, there is a story. Look at the names in the list and their meaning.

Adam	Man
Seth	Appointed
Enosh	Mortal
Kenan	Sorrow
Mahalalel	The blessed God
Jared	Shall come down
Enoch	Teaching
Methuselah	His death shall bring
Lamech	The despairing
Noah	Comfort, Rest

Now read just their meaning and you get the gospel story of the Messiah.(3)

2) On some occasions *God gave the name* of the child to the parents, as in the cases of Ishmael (God hears - Genesis 16:11), Isaac (Laughter - Genesis 17:19), and Jesus (God with us - Matthew 1:21). Each name tells a story.

There is a very interesting verse below. I have shown it in two translations. Does God give us our names before we are ever born? I have been perplexed in reading this verse and it seems to answer in the affirmative. If so, it's a "wow" verse. The prophet Isaiah wrote,

"Listen to me you islands, hear this you distant nations: Before I was born the Lord called me; **from my mother's womb He has spoken my name**" (Isaiah 49:1, NIV).

Listen to Me, O islands, and pay attention, you peoples from afar. The Lord called Me from the womb; From the body of My mother **He** named Me. (NASB)

3) At other times children were named based *on what was happening in the lives of the parents*. Leah is an example of life change.

Both Leah and her sister Rachel were married to the same man, Jacob. Because Jacob favored Rachael over her, Leah longed to be loved. She was able to conceive and give Jacob sons, which she mistakenly thought would bring her fulfillment. Each son's name was a derivative of seeking her husband's love: Reuben (surely now my husband will love me), Simeon (I am unloved) and Levi (my husband will be attached to me). Then we notice a change in Leah with the birth name of her fourth son. Judah means "I will praise God". What happened? She stopped seeking love from a man to thanking God that she was loved by Him. Amazing!

Joseph gives another example of a parent's life change reflected in the naming of his children. As you recall, Joseph was betrayed by his brothers, sold as a slave into Egypt, and put in an Egyptian prison for something he didn't do. When he was finally released, he was made second in command under Pharaoh. He later married an Egyptian woman and had two sons. The names of his sons tell his story. He named them *Manasseh*, which means "God has made me forget the pain of my father's household," and *Ephraim*, "God has made me prosper" (I can go on, my future is secure). In the New Testament, Paul picks up on this theology by saying, "Forgetting what lies behind and reaching forward to what lies ahead, I press on toward the goal for the prize of the upward call of God in Christ Jesus" (Philippians 3:13). This is a clear statement of what Joseph testified to in the naming of his sons. In order to have an Ephraim (positive future) we need to first have a Manasseh (putting the past away).

4) God also changed names on occasion, to mark a *significant event in the life of a person*. Abram (father) became Abraham (father of a multitude - Genesis 17:5), Sarai (princess) became Sarah (mother of nations - Genesis 17:15).

Jacob means "supplanter" or "deceiver"; he was given this name because of what happened at his birth (Genesis 25:26). Jacob fulfilled much of that meaning by the life he lived. But when God wrestled with him, He changed his name to Israel (Genesis 32:28) which means "wrestles with God."

The name Israel has meaning for the nation (and all of humanity). It is no accident that God gave this name to a nation who continually wrestles with Him, both ancient and modern, as well as to generally depict all of human nature. Trials in life give a clear example of our wrestling with Him. Whether severe, short, or long, we do some heavy-duty wrestling with God. When the trial is lessened, we quickly forget that we have wrestled at all. God welcomes these wrestling matches as a way to get across to our stubborn hearts that He loves us too much to let us get away with sin in our lives.

5) *Cities were also given meaning-laden names.* For example, Bethlehem means "house of bread," Bethel means "house of God," and Jerusalem means "city of peace." Many cities in biblical times were named because of what took place there or for what the citizens wanted their city to be known for.

6) Throughout Scripture *God's names* are given utmost importance. At times He tells us His name, at other times people gave Him names. You will encounter several of His names in the book of Ruth. His names show His character and range from the highest pinnacle of holiness to the intricate care of an individual human being. When you know His diverse and multitudinal names, you fall in love with His character.

The Importance of Names in Ruth

Names are connected to the story they tell. It was so in biblical times, and it is still so today. Moms- and dads-to-be take great pains in coming up with the perfect name for their child. Some choose a family name to honor a parent, grandparent, or favorite relative. Others choose the name of a notable person from history. Choosing a name is an important decision because names have meaning and will tell a story for years to come.

As we approach the book of Ruth, remember that the meaning of names is important to the overall story God is telling. The spotlight will be on a family who is surrounded by darkness. Learn what their names mean and how those meanings help tell the story. The very first verse is a *hinge* to the book of Judges. The spotlight is on a family who is surrounded by darkness, demanding a human king.

God never leaves Himself without a witness to His power and care over a people, no matter how evil the society might be. There will always be those who follow Him wholeheartedly in spite of the philosophical clamoring around them. This was that kind of family and that kind of witness. The name Elimelech proves it—*our God is King!*

Stay or Go?

Elimelech married a woman named Naomi, which means "pleasant and lovely." (She appears to have been pleasant, kind, appealing, and sweet.) Both Elimelech and Naomi came from the tribe of Judah, one of the largest tribes in the land. It would not have been uncommon for them to be related, and may have been first, second, or third cousins. Because most people did not move far from their families, they were probably born and raised in close proximity. And according to custom, their parents would have picked them as mates while Naomi was young.

During their early marriage they had two sons, Mahlon, meaning "puny," and Chileon, meaning "pining." Now, what parents in their right minds would name their children puny and pining without a reason?

The first verse of chapter one gives us a clue: there was a famine in the land. With food in short supply, Naomi may not have received proper nutrition during her pregnancies. She may not have been in good health or perhaps she had the boys very close together, her body not having time to recover between births. The boys themselves may have been premature and, therefore, were not normal weight at birth.

Did these names have still deeper meaning? Did they symbolize what was happening nationally? Corruption was rampant. Evil was pervasive. The spiritual climate of Israel was puny and the people would have been pining for a better life. Whatever the reason, the boys' names indicate that times were not good.

Famines were often brought about by God in response to disobedience among His people. This was certainly the case during the reign of the judges. Yet Matthew 5:45 says, "For He causes His sun to rise on the evil and the good, and sends rain on the righteous and the unrighteous." Famines affected everyone, the evil and the good, the righteous and the unrighteous. Good people suffer the consequence of poor judgment on the part of the ungodly. This is a clear teaching of Scripture.

As any loving parents would, Elimelech and Naomi wanted to find food for their hungry family. Some scholars conclude that they were in disobedience to God when they left Bethlehem. After all, they were in the promised-land. And if we look at their decision to leave from a purely human viewpoint, we might conclude that God would have met their needs had they stayed in Bethlehem. However, in light of the sovereignty of God, as they prayed for wisdom, it is not a stretch to think God led them to leave Bethlehem to find food elsewhere.

As I said in the previous chapter, I believe the books of Judges and Ruth are mirrored opposites. In Judges disobedience and selfishness abounds, whereas in Ruth there is faith, surrender and obedience. If Elimelech and Naomi were God-followers, as I believe they were, could it have been the sovereignty of God that led them to sojourn (not permanently move) to another land? After all, they didn't sell their land. They were planning to return when the time was right.

If it was disobedient for them to sojourn, then we should contemplate other biblical passages where a temporary move to another country would have also been outside of God's will. For example, Jacob and his sons and their families went to sojourn in Egypt. Why? They were hungry! Remember that Joseph was already there—sent ahead by God—and invited his family to move to where he and an ample supply of food were (Genesis 45:9; Acts 7:14). Did God lead them there? Absolutely. He led them there and He would lead them out. Another passage concerns Mary and Joseph. An angel told them to flee Bethlehem and go to Egypt to avoid the premature killing of Jesus (Matthew 2:13). In both cases these people clearly moved within God's will. In the case of Elimelech and Naomi, we have no record of why they moved except for the famine. Is God sovereign over moves in the lives of His biblical characters and in our lives in the present? I believe He is.

The Sovereignty of God

God loves adventure. He is sovereign over the events of people and the events of nations. *Sovereignty* means that God, as the ruler of the universe, has the right to do whatever He pleases. Furthermore, He is in complete control over everything that happens. God in His sovereignty would use Elimelech and Naomi's move for His higher purpose.

The irony of the gospel, and indeed the strength of the book of Ruth, is that God chooses differently than we would. He takes the weak and the ordinary to do His will. He chose a willing family and led them to a country where He was planning an awesome work that they knew nothing about. Remember, God is building His kingdom. How does He pull the Gentile nations into His kingdom work?

Did God have something or someone in mind of which Elimelech and Naomi knew nothing? God had reasons for leading them to pick up and leave the only security and comfort of home and family. For them the decision was not easy. For the Hebrew people to move out of their secure familial environment would have been unusual and not without first wrestling with God. But they were compelled to think in terms of food for their boys, and they knew that the surrounding countries were not experiencing the famine that Israel was.

If their boys were in need of food, it was even more urgent for Elimelech and Naomi to seek sustenance elsewhere. Parents will do anything humanly possible to feed their children. Ironically, they left Bethlehem, the House of Bread, in search of bread. Either they had heard that Moab with its lush farmland was the place to go, or they just set out in search of an area where there was the best possibility of surviving. Moab was a narrow strip of fertile, well-watered land east of the Dead Sea (present-day Jordan). The land was good for farming and raising livestock. Elimelech owned land in the area of Bethlehem, but because of either drought or marauders, his land lay unproductive.

Though Moab had once fought against Israel (Judges 3:12–30), at this time the nations were at peace. So it stands to reason why Elimelech and Naomi went in that direction. If there was no food in their homeland, maybe God would direct them to where their needs would be met. These parents journeyed out of their comfort zone to a people they didn't know. Did they have fear? Of course they did. Did they question their own motives? Probably. Did they wrestle with God? Undoubtedly. Human beings always wrestle with the what-ifs of moving. They would have been no exception.

Settling in Moab

When coming into the land of Moab, they were probably greeted in a small village with bread and wine. That was the custom of hospitality. We know from the book of Genesis that Abraham was greeted by a neighboring king, Melchizedek, with bread and wine (Genesis 14:18). This was both a custom of greeting and a sign of friendship. Elimelech and Naomi were welcomed or they would not have stayed.

It must have felt good for them to settle down in an area where the boys would have food and where they could mature into young men. I imagine when leaving Bethlehem, Elimelech had assured Naomi that it would be temporary, just long enough to have food on the table and no worries about tomorrow's supply.

If God is sovereign, and He is, He was the One who led them to the exact location of settlement. And I wonder, could it have been Ruth's parents who welcomed them with bread and wine when they arrived? My thinking is this: Ruth was probably a young girl in the same neighborhood when the family of Elimelech came to town. And to look ahead in the story, it would have been rare for Mahlon and Chilion to marry women whom their families did not know. Granted, we can't be sure exactly when and how the families met, but we do know that God brought them together.

Naomi the Storyteller

Ruth's and Orpha's families were no doubt well acquainted (these two girls would later marry the sons of Elimelech and Naomi). They may have been related, as people in villages often were. These two little girls felt a tug on their hearts toward this wonderful lady, Naomi, and may have gone in afternoons to listen to her stories and snack on honey cakes. Asking permission from their mothers, they may have heard, "Run along child, but be home for supper. You still have work to do." And they would go, and they would listen. They would have Naomi repeat stories that are still enjoyed by children in Sunday school classes and Bible clubs today.

Naomi, being from the tribe of Judah, would have told them about the sovereign God who created the world, the sun, and the moon. How different from the stories of their gods, gods of the sun and of the moon. Naomi would tell of Adam and Eve, of Noah and his fantastic boat and the flood, the Tower of Babel and beginning of languages. She would tell stories about Judah, her tribe's patriarch, and his eleven brothers and their tribes. She would tell them of Joseph and his coat of many colors, and of Moses leading the Israelite slaves out of Egypt, and of course the parting of the Red Sea. So fantastic were her stories that these girls would wonder at the God of the Hebrews. Their gods had done nothing so astounding as this new God.

Of course, she would tell of the wandering in the wilderness for forty years and the Tabernacle with its cloud covering it by day and the fire lighting it by night. Naomi would have told them about Joshua conquering the land of Canaan and how their own country of Moab had played into that story.

Naomi had many stories to tell these young listeners, and I'm sure they sat with rapt attention. Through it all, little Ruth and Orpah came to love this foreign woman and they began to fall in love with her God. To Naomi, God was real and personable and cared about her and her family. He cared about two little Moabite girls whose heartstrings He had been tugging, and wooing to Himself.

When you are in a dark place, you either burn brighter or you slowly dim. Elimelech and Naomi were in a dark place, a pagan country with no family and no familiar place of worship. Would they be lights to those who sit in darkness, or would they melt into the culture? They began to burn brighter and brighter.

In their own homeland the stories had grown so familiar that they were not exciting anymore. In Bethlehem, anything spiritual was boring. It was old news. After all, even supposedly good men were doing evil and calling it good. In God's sovereignty He took this family out of their comfort zone to see what they were made of. And they passed the test.

The Wooing of Young Ruth

God had another purpose that was not known to Naomi; He was going to use her to woo and win a little girl named Ruth who would change history. You see, Elimelech *had* to go to Moab. Naomi *had* to disciple young children in Moab. One young girl was to be singled out.

Naomi may have discovered that these young girls in this village were hungry for what she had. They saw in her a pleasant and lovely woman with graces they needed and kindness that won their hearts. Yes, I believe they spent many hours with this woman before the next event took place. They must have been impressed with the whole family. They watched father and sons work together in the fields and in the village. They watched Naomi care for her family. Yes, what Naomi had, they wanted. They loved her stories, but more than that they were falling in love with her God.

I have had a similar experience in my own life. Don and I, along with others, planted our first church in Dallas and also began our marriage ministry, Christian Family Life. Several years later we moved to Little Rock, Arkansas. It was there that we planted our second Fellowship Bible Church, one I loved very much. We also began another ministry called FamilyLife. I loved our time in Little Rock so much that I never wanted to leave. Within three or four years of our time there we were asked to come to Washington, DC, to minister to congressional couples. I didn't want to go and really drug my feet. Don strongly felt led to move, so in obedience, I agreed. But I cried all the way to DC with our belongings and kids in tow.

We stayed in DC for ten wonderful years, planting four more churches and building many lasting friendships. My four children grew to maturity with two going to college in Virginia.

Were we in God's will in moving? At the time I questioned it. But within a short period I realized God was in the move. We loved the DC area. Both our marriage ministry and our church planting ministry flourished. Fond memories accrued. We were right where God wanted us. We were in the center of His will.

I believe the same holds true for Elimelech and Naomi. They were a spiritually oriented family in the center of God's will, being moved by Him to go to Moab. The decision Elimelech made mattered – they didn't know it but a little girl named Ruth was waiting for the change that would ultimately affect her life *and ours*. And the decisions Ruth made mattered for eternity. The decisions we make also matter. They have consequences long after we are gone. What we do matters. What we say matters. How we live our life matters. It matters to God and it matters to people who follow after us.

Chapter Discussion

1.   Explain how names are significant to this story. What is important about the name "Israel?"

2.   What is the meaning of your name? Write out a short story of your life using your names. (My example is written below – be brief).

3.   How does the sovereignty of God play into this story?

4.   Has there been a time in your life where you can pinpoint God's sovereignty at work (in relationships, moves, locations, etc.)? Describe results of decisions made.

5.   Give your own thoughts concerning the relationship between Ruth and Orpah.

6.   Read Psalm 139. Describe the sovereignty of God in light of this chapter.

Example:

(My first name is a derivative of *Sarah* and means "princess". My middle name is *Renee* and means "reborn." So I guess you could say I am a "princess reborn." I accept that I am a princess because I have entered the household of God, being reborn as His child. It's actually quite fun to visualize.

I was Sally Renee Hill for twenty-seven years. That part of my story is connected to my original name. I grew up with a non-believing father who was a negative and critical man. My father never told me he loved me nor did he tell me I was pretty. I longed for that from *any* man.

When I met Don, and knew he was to be my husband, neither of us understood how to love an imperfect person. We had a very rocky beginning as both of us brought our own baggage into the marriage. For the last forty-seven years I have been Sally Meredith. Connected to that name has been a new and unfolding story. Don began to study Scripture to answer the question: If God created marriage, could He make it work? In the process, Don learned to love me like I had always wanted to be loved and cherished. I learned to respect him for the man God created him to be. Our marriage continues to be led by the faith commitments we discovered early in marriage. In fact, we wrote a book called *Two Becoming One,* based on the faith principles we learned from God's Word. Those principles changed not only our lives but countless others who have followed God's directions.

With my new name I have had four children and eleven grandchildren. Together Don and I have helped plant eight churches, planted several ministries, led Bible studies, taught on marriage, spoken together, lived together, laughed together, and cried together. Life has had its twists and turns but God has been faithful and today we are more in love with Him and with each other than at any time in our lives.)

Chapter 3

Your Life and Death Matter to God

Then Elimelech, Naomi's husband, died; and she was left with her two sons. And they took for themselves Moabite women as wives; the name of the one was Orpah and the name of the other Ruth. And they lived there about ten years.
—Ruth 1:3–4

Losing a husband is a terrible thing. It must have been especially troubling to Naomi for this to happen in a foreign land. She didn't have lifelong friends and family surrounding her. It must have been a very perplexing time. How could she go on? What should she do? Should she and her two sons go home to Bethlehem? They must have discussed this around the dinner table, perhaps talking deep into the nights. Stay or go? Her sons may have expressed their desires and she told them of hers. Obviously they chose to stay.

Mahlon, being the oldest, would have had the responsibility to care for his aging mother, yet they all would have lived together while both her sons were still single. Perhaps the names of Ruth and Orpah came up in conversation from time to time.

Sometime during the ten years that Naomi lived in Moab, she gained influence in the lives of these two young women. Both girls grew to love her deeply. They had also put their trust in Yahweh, the God of the Hebrews, for Naomi approved of the marriages to her two sons. That would have been unlikely given the laws of Moses where marriage was forbidden with pagan women unless they became converts.

23

Naomi's Thinking Process and Actions

It would have been Naomi who broached the subject of marriage with the parents of Ruth and Orpah. The parents always picked mates for their children. Was it a difficult discussion between the families, I wonder? It was not unlawful for Moabites to intermarry with other tribes, but it was unusual. There were no laws against it, and the approval may have come easily if the families had been friends. These two girls had adopted Naomi's God as their own and consented to become proselytes and raise their children as Hebrews.

Naomi must have enjoyed the weddings! Women do, you know. Life was good and life was bright. Ruth and Orpah were honored to marry brothers who would lead them into more knowledge of this one true God. Their new mother-in-law was already special to them, now she would be family.

Remembering Rahab

In giving her approval of these two Moabite women, perhaps Naomi had her own ancestor Rahab in the back of her mind. At the outset of the conquest of Canaan, the Israelites came first to the city of Jericho, where they were given a battle plan from God to conquer the city. One of the inhabitants was a young prostitute named Rahab who had heard of the God of the Israelites. She knew the story of the crossing of the Red Sea and of the obedience of these strange people to their strange God. She had heard the stories of His power and strength. She was curious, and when the Israelite warriors came to her town, she did everything she could to help them.

Here is her statement of faith *before* she and her family were saved.

> Now before [the Hebrew spies] lay down, [Rahab] came up to
> them on the roof, and said to the men, "I know that the LORD
> has given you the land, and that the terror of you has fallen on

us, and that all the inhabitants of the land have melted away before you. For we have heard how the LORD dried up the water of the Red Sea before you when you came out of Egypt, and what you did to the two kings of the Amorites who were beyond the Jordan, to Sihon and Og, whom you utterly destroyed. When we heard it, our hearts melted and no courage remained in any man any longer because of you; for the LORD your God, He is God in heaven above and on earth beneath. Now therefore, please swear to me by the LORD, since I have dealt kindly with you, that you also will deal kindly with my father's household, and give me a pledge of truth. (Joshua 2:8–12)

We know from the biblical account in Joshua 2 and 6 that Rahab's faith in Jehovah saved her and her family from slaughter. Later she even married one of the conquering warriors, Salmon. Her story would be well known among the Israelites for generations. Her pre-faith reputation was legend as was her saving faith after conversion.

Rahab had acknowledged that "He is God [Elohim] in heaven above and on the earth beneath" (Joshua 2:11) even though she was raised believing in numerous gods. She exhibited a change of heart and believed in this one true God. She also calls God Yahweh (LORD) showing her faith in Him before she even knew Him. Through her act of obedience, she helped the Israelites conquer her own city. She and her immediate family were spared while the rest of Jericho perished in the assault.

After Rahab and her family went with the Israelites, she married into one of the predominant tribes, the tribe of Judah. Her genealogy is listed in the chronicles of Israel (1 Chronicles 2:11), the book of Ruth (4:21), the lineage of Jesus (Matthew 1:5), and listed as a woman of faith (Hebrews 11:31).

After Rahab's conversion and inclusion into the people of God, she must have had a continuing influence upon her children and grandchildren. Her son's name, Boaz, spoke volumes about the faith of this family; it means "in Him is strength." Rahab's conversion was solid; her faith impenetrable.

When I meet this woman in heaven I might greet her by saying, "Oh, you're Rahab, the Harlot!" and then catch myself. She will laugh and say, "Yes, I am." I will then want to ask if she had ever wanted that title—the Harlot—to be dropped. She may say, "Yes, but with that title came my unbelievable inclusion in the covenant promises of Yahweh. I became a chosen one! So, no. It's okay to remember that title, for God is a God of second chances."

Yes, God welcomed into the culture of His chosen people anyone who put their trust in Him. This included the young Canaanite Rahab and, as we will see, the young Moabite Ruth.

Barren Wombs

Neither Ruth nor Orpah conceived children. The timing wasn't yet right, and neither was the DNA. The Sovereign God of Israel—the One who opens and closes wombs—was on a mission. He had to send a family from the tribe of Judah to Moab to collect a young girl named Ruth.

The story is building.

Ruth would have spent many hours with Naomi, not only before marriage, but after as well. Naomi would have lived with the eldest son, Mahlon and his wife, Ruth. We are not told much about their marriage, only that they lived there ten years. Some of those years were no doubt before marriage and some were after. In spite of losing her husband, Naomi had four people who loved her and walked through the grieving process with her.

Ruth and Mahlon would have been responsible to meet whatever needs Naomi would have had after the death of Elimelech. It is clear from the rest of the book that Ruth had a very special relationship with her mother-in-law. This was unusual in the culture of her day. Mothers adored and catered to their sons but only tolerated their daughters-in-law. So we see in this story that Naomi was unique. Her relationship with these young women was personal and loving. Because she loved them, they were attracted to her God.

As a little girl in Moab, Ruth would have grown up in a home where many gods were worshipped, but Israel had one God. In Ruth's culture, it was common to sacrifice children on altars to appease their gods. Ruth must have been comforted by the fact that when she married Mahlon, no children of hers would ever be sacrificed. She must have also noticed the different way women were treated—not as chattel, but loved by the husband. She must have observed that sweet relationship in the marriage of Elimelech and Naomi. That was different from her culture where men married numerous wives who were often demeaned, abused, or used for selfish lusts.

Naomi had already lost her lover, her provider, her friend, Elimelech. She had been wounded and had grieved deeply. But in His wonderful sovereignty, God had provided her sons with two wonderful women whom she loved as if they were her very own daughters. She could go on. With these marriages, she had not lost sons, but had gained friends in their wives.

Naomi now longed for a legacy. She waited patiently for the conception and births of grandchildren. But no children graced either home. To outward appearances both Ruth and Orpah were barren. How difficult that must have been for the families. Hadn't God promised that if they followed Him, He would bless the fruit of their wombs? Month followed month, and still no swollen bellies with the joy of movement. Tears came. Maybe next month . . .

Severe Storm

Piercing suddenly into these quiet lives of normalcy came one of the most severe trials any woman ever has to face. "Then both Mahlon and Chilion also died, and [Naomi] was bereft of her two children and her husband" (Ruth 1:5). Oh my! What did they die of, I wonder. Did they perish together in some catastrophic accident? Did they die days apart, months apart? Wouldn't you like to know that story? I would. But it's not central to the rest of this story. Somehow, Ruth must get to Bethlehem to fulfill what God has in store for her. All the pieces are falling into place (we know the end of the story), but let's not get ahead. Let's not move too quickly past Naomi's deep pain.

Children are supposed to outlive their parents. Why would God take both of her boys? The storm that raged in her soul knew no bounds. Where was God? Did He not care? Hadn't she put all her trust in Him and didn't it now seem He had failed her? Life was not worth living without her husband and her children. How could she go on?

What do you do when the storms of life ravage your soul? What do you do when sleep comes only from exhaustion? How do you eat when nothing tastes good? Broken hearts mend painfully slow. All her dreams were wrapped up in her sons. Now those dreams lay shattered around her like shards of glass. Every memory brought sharp pain.

Storms in nature have a purpose. Heavy rains go deep into the soil to make roots stronger. Trees grow taller and thicker, better prepared for the next storm. Without storms, the trees would have shallow roots and could be blown over with the slightest wind. Without deep water, the tree would grow fast and spongy. It takes hard storms to anchor a tree and cause it to grow straight and tall and able to endure through time.

Could it be that the storms of our lives are intended to cause us to grow deeper and stronger? Each storm is important to the growth of our character. Each one builds upon the last. Each storm anchors us to the One who holds tomorrow.

The Death of Dreams

There is a profound and puzzling passage in James 1:2–4 that says: "Consider it all joy, my brethren, when you encounter various trials, knowing that the testing of your faith produces endurance. And let endurance have its perfect result, so that you may be perfect and complete, lacking in nothing."

Consider it joy? No one considers trials a joy. Instead, we question. We falter. We ask God why, and the heavens are silent. But Scripture is for our edification; and as we submit, God will, in time, give us perspective of the trial. He may never show us why, but He will always give us a different perspective that will help us in our journey toward the future. God's love for us is so deep, so lasting, and so strong that He purposes only good for us. Trials cause us to grow and mature and become more caring for others. Not all trials will be the same in intensity or length. But each one is important to the ongoing process of changing us into the image of God's dear Son.

I will venture to say that it was many years later when Naomi realized the incalculable and numerous trials she had come through. She certainly didn't consider what she was going through to be *joy*. Far from it. We don't really know what trials Elimelech and Naomi went through in Bethlehem before the famine. The birth of puny babies must have been a worrisome trial, as they may not have expected their boys to survive. And moving is always stress-filled, whether to the next town or, in this case, the next country. Meeting new neighbors, settling in to a different culture, finding a job, new housing, and just daily living all must have taken a toll.

This family survived and enjoyed Moab and the people they met there. But the next trial, that of Elimelech's death, was much deeper. Naomi still had her sons, though. But when they died, her trial was the blackest of blacks. Each preceding trial prepared her for what was to come.

People have said that God will never gives us more than we can bear. But I disagree. He does give us more than we can bear. At times He brings us to the breaking point to see what is in our heart. (Surely Naomi was there, at her breaking point.) Trials are never meant to be borne alone, yet often we feel so very much alone. God will take us through what is beyond our ability to bear. He will lift us up. At times He will carry us because we cannot put one foot in front of the other.

Footprints in the Sand
by Mary Stevenson

One night I dreamed a dream.
As I was walking along the beach with my Lord
Across the dark sky flashed scenes from my life.
For each scene, I noticed two sets of footprints in the sand,
One belonging to me and one to my Lord.
After the last scene of my life flashed before me,
I looked back at the footprints in the sand.
I noticed that at many times along the path of my life,
Especially at the very lowest and saddest times,
There was only one set of footprints.
This really troubled me, so I asked the Lord about it.
"Lord, you said once I decided to follow you,
You'd walk with me all the way.
But I noticed that during the saddest
And most troublesome times of my life,
There was only one set of footprints.
I don't understand why, when I needed You the most,

You would leave me."
He whispered, "My precious child,
I love you and will never leave you.
Never, ever, during your trials and testings.
When you saw only one set of footprints,
It was then that I carried you." (4)

Ruth and Orpah had lost their husbands and were also grieving, but Naomi was in deep anguish. Oh, she knew her daughters-in-law were grieving, but her pain was so intense, so deep, so excruciating that she was unable to see beyond her own pain. Naomi's identity was wrapped up in her husband and sons. She began the period of wrestling with her God. Her dreams of lifelong companionship? Shattered. Her hopes for grandchildren? Gone. Being taken care of her in her old age? Wouldn't happen. The death of dreams is so incredibly devastating that to curl up and die would be a welcomed relief. Why does God test us so? What does He know that we don't?

Hear what Scripture has to say about testing.

You shall remember all the way which the LORD your God has led you. . . . *that He might humble you, testing you*, to know what was in your heart, whether you would keep His commandments or not. . . . that He might humble you and that He might test you, *to do good* for you in the end. (Deuteronomy 8:2, 16, emphasis added)

Trials are used in our lives to cause inward growth and humility. Trials give us tenderness, caring, and the capacity to comfort others. Trials stamp out pride. God knows just what trial will be good for us at any given time. His desire is that we grow strong, not in ourselves but in our trust of Him. He is sovereign over every detail of life. He is sovereign over every trial. He knows what He is bringing into our lives and why. He may not cause all trials, but He reigns supreme over all circumstances. There is no sin, no trial, no suffering, no sickness, no identity beyond the healing touch of God.

Widowhood

The 2000 US Census revealed some staggering statistics about widowhood.

- 85–90% of women will outlive their husbands.
- 75% of women are single when they die.
- 50% of women who reach the age of 65 will outlive their husbands by 15 years.
- 80–90% of women will be responsible for their household income at some point in their adult lives.
- 90% of women will end up living alone or with extended family members.
- In 2000 there were 12 million widows in the United States.
- 1 million Americans are widowed each year, 69% are women

Most women will experience widowhood. It is important to understand that God has life and purpose for the widow. Several of my good friends have gone through this grieving experience and have come out on the other side full of life and kingdom-building purpose. Don and I have made it our practice to include widows in many of our activities. Why? Because they are our friends whom we love just as much as we did when we were friends as couples.

The book of Ruth has a great deal to say about widows and how God pursues, protects, and provides for them in an almost relentless manner. He gives instructions to believers to take care of the orphans and widows (Exodus 22:22; Isaiah 1:17; 1 Timothy 5:3). It is the responsibility of the church and families to care for them. We are not to reject them but to wrap them into our own family structure so they will feel part of the Body just as they did when they were married. God still has a purpose and a ministry for widows. His kingdom building doesn't end when a person finds herself alone.

Years ago two very special women were part of our second church plant. One was a young single woman and the other an older widow. These two women literally were the backbone of this new church. They had an incredible ministry that lasted till the older one went to be with the Lord (thirty years of ministry after her husband died) and the younger one took on the women's ministry and then married a widower. With her husband she became a mother to his children and then a grandmother. God doesn't put widows out to pasture and we shouldn't either.

The Wounded Go Home

As Naomi pondered her fate one dark and lonely night, she knew it was time to go home. Don't the wounded always want to go home? Whether a child is hurt on the playground or a soldier is wounded on the battlefield, home offers them comfort and a sense of belonging. The feel of familiar arms and the assurance that everything will be all right is so needed. Yes, Naomi wanted to go home. God had been in the move to Moab, and now He was putting in her heart and mind to go home to Bethlehem. The famine had been over for quite some time. Surely she could find a suitable home back among her own people. There was nothing in Moab to keep her any longer.

> Then she arose with her daughters-in-law that she might return from the land of Moab, for she had heard in the land of Moab that the LORD had visited His people in giving them food. So she departed from the place where she was, and her two daughters-in-law with her; and they went on the way to return to the land of Judah. (Ruth 1:6–7)

Upon reaching the decision, Naomi told Ruth and Orpah that she was returning to Bethlehem. They would go with her, and so began preparing for the journey. After all, she had done so much for them, this was the least they could do for her. They understood her and loved her. They would make sure she made it to Bethlehem. They would help care for her. I don't believe these two women gave much thought for themselves at this point. They were thinking of Naomi and doing what they could for their friend, mentor, and much-loved mother-in-law.

There are two routes they could have taken. If they lived in northern Moab, the journey to Bethlehem would have been some eighty or more miles through different territories above the Dead Sea and down to Bethlehem. If they lived in southern Moab, they would have taken a much shorter route, south along the Dead Sea and then north to Bethlehem. Walking only a few miles each day would have taken a fairly long time either way. They would be at the mercy of other travelers as well as the villages they passed through.

What Am I Doing?

Early in the journey it dawned on Naomi how selfish she had been. Her daughters-in-law had quickly packed and left with her, and she suddenly realized the magnitude of what she had asked of them. She determined that she just couldn't take them away from the only home they had ever known, so she gave them her blessing to go back to their homes in Moab.

She wanted them to be happy and she knew she had no means to make that happen. She would encourage them to go back to the familiar. Oh, she would miss them terribly. They were her only family now. Tears of sorrow coursed down her weathered cheeks as she thought of their parting. But she had no right to ask them to go to her people and homeland. It wasn't fair. She knew she could go on alone and the Almighty would sustain her. She was not afraid.

Chapter Discussion

1. Why would Naomi have stayed on in Moab after the death of Elimelech?

2. Describe the importance of Rahab's story to understanding the book of Ruth.

3. Describe a storm in your own life that became helpful to you or to others through you.

4. Why would God want us to "consider it all joy" (James 1:2-4) when going through trials?

5. Read Deuteronomy 8:2, 16. What is the purpose of trials?

6. How can you, as an individual, or your church better support and care for widows in your congregation?

Chapter 4

Your Commitments Matter to God

And Naomi said to her two daughters-in-law, "Go, return each of you to her mother's house. May the LORD deal kindly with you as you have dealt with the dead and with me. May the LORD grant that you may find rest, each in the house of her [future] husband." Then she kissed them, and they lifted up their voices and wept.
—Ruth 1:8–9

Blessings to Return

Spoken blessings can be found throughout the book of Ruth; there are fourteen in all. Blessings flow from relationship—woman to woman, man to woman, man to man, friend to friend—and giving them is an important part of our calling as God-followers. Blessings begin with "May the Lord . . ." or "May you be blessed of the Lord." A past blessing is often included (for example, "As you have . . .") as well as a blessing for the future ("May the Lord grant you . . ."). Blessings are usually given when something has been completed or a new chapter of life is beginning. (See Appendix 1 for a further description as well as information on blessing ceremonies.)

What a tender scene we see as Naomi not only urges Ruth and Orpah to leave her, but also gives them her blessing as they go. Basically, she gave them her blessing to leave her, return to their families, and to remarry. They had blessed her life and her sons' lives. They could part from her with her full blessing upon their futures.

Ruth 1:10–13 records more of this conversation.

And they said to her, "No, but we will surely return with you to your people." But Naomi said, "Return my daughters. Why should you go with me? Have I yet sons in my womb, that they may be your husbands? Return my daughters! Go, for I am too old to have a husband. If I said I have hope, if I should even have a husband tonight and also bear sons, would you therefore wait until they were grown? Would you therefore refrain from marrying? No, my daughters; for it is harder for me than for you, for the hand of the LORD has gone forth against me."

Levirate Law of Marriage Explained

Naomi was recalling for these two young women the Israelite cultural practice of Levirate marriage, stated in the Law of Moses (Leviticus 19:9–10; 23:22). Clearly Naomi had already taught this law to them because she doesn't elaborate on it nor do they ask questions. They understood. Naomi also stated the obvious, that she was past childbearing even if she remarried. She knew what an honor it had been to have a husband and children, and she wanted nothing less for them. She wanted them to remarry and have children. They were young and that was still possible, but not with her.

The custom of Levirate marriage was this: When a man died and he was childless (the case here) the unmarried brother of the dead man would marry the widow and she would bear children. Therefore the genealogy would continue for the family. If a brother was not available (the case here), then the closest relative would step in to marry her. Naomi, being past menopause, would have no more sons; therefore, Ruth and Orpah would not even be eligible for a Levirate marriage. Both women completely understood this law and the implications.

Orpah: Believer or Not?

> And they lifted up their voices and wept again; and Orpah kissed her mother-in-law, but Ruth clung to her. Then she said, "Behold, your sister-in-law has gone back to her people and her gods; return after your sister-in-law." (Ruth 1:14–15)

Ruth did not leave, but Orpah did. She wept, kissed Naomi and Ruth and began her journey back home to Moab. These three women grieved the parting of their friendship for they knew they probably would never see one another again. I believe Ruth and Orpah were childhood friends. Their hearts must have torn when they parted. Orpah would see Ruth's family. Ruth would not. Orpah would see their friends again. Ruth would not.

I wonder: Did Orpah go back and melt again into her culture and worship the gods she was raised with? Was her faith more fragile than Ruth's? Was Orpah fearful of going to a strange people and country? We are not told.

At this point Orpah drops out of the narrative. She is not part of the ongoing story of Ruth and Naomi. But if she truly had fallen in love with Israel's God, the one true God, then we will see her in heaven. And what a story she might tell. Revelation 5:9 says that there will be "people from every tribe, every tongue, and every people and every nation" worshipping Him in whom they put their trust. Will Orpah be there? I hope so. Will there be others from Moab? Did Naomi witness to other children in their village? Did Orpah go home with even more conviction of her faith? By returning she missed out on the blessings of God's covenant with Israel. However, she did not miss out on knowing about Israel's God and maybe even knowing Him personally.

Was Orpah as a person important to the God of Israel? You bet she was, as was her country of Moab. Otherwise, God would not have taken the time to send "missionaries" to her land. He could have left her out of the narrative altogether, but He didn't. She is there for a reason. If she is in heaven I will certainly want to hear her story, won't you?

Ruth's Covenant Statement

Ruth now turns to Naomi, her favorite person on earth. The one who had taught and mentored her. The one who had shown her the one true God. The one to whom she could turn when she had spiritual questions.

I believe it came as no surprise when Ruth made such a strong and beautiful statement of loyalty. Naomi knew what kind of woman Ruth was. She had grown to love her in Moab. She had watched her in marriage to her eldest son. They had become closer each day as Ruth grew spiritually. Yet she may have wondered if Bethlehem would test the love of this Moabite daughter and if they would remain close. But I don't believe anything could have come between them. Time had been spent, hearts tested, loyalty cemented.

The statement Ruth made to Naomi is filled with meaning. Some women could make this statement to their mother, but not to their mother-in-law without understanding the background of such a commitment. Her words are full of the knowledge of Yahweh and Hebrew ways. She spoke with the force of one who is a seasoned believer.

> "Don't urge me to leave you or turn back from following you; for where you go I will go, and where you lodge I will lodge. Your people shall be my people, and your God, my God [Elohim]. Where you die I will die, and there I will be buried. May the LORD [Yahweh] do to me, and worse, if anything but death parts you and me." (Ruth 1:16–17)

Ruth *couldn't* go back to paganism. She had already severed those ties with her own family, probably on account of her new found faith in a different God. She spoke of Elohim, maker of heaven and earth. Whenever a pagan worshipper turned to the God of the Hebrews they changed their title of worship from numerous gods to one true God, maker of heaven and earth. This is the same name for God used in Genesis 1:1, "In the beginning, [Elohim] created the heavens and the earth." In other words, Ruth was declaring that "your Elohim is my Elohim." By turning to Elohim, she broke ties with her pagan background. This would be a statement of a new believer. It's a conversion statement.

And there's more.

When Ruth says "may the LORD," she uses another statement of even deeper faith. God had now become her personal Master, Judge, and Lord. This is the name *Yahweh*, and it is the personal name of God. Using it implies submission to an unseen power that rules not only the universe but her life as well. This name for God indicates mature faith that has stood the test of time and submission to God as the only self-existing One. He was the only God who existed. She submitted to no other gods.

Later we will see her use the name *El Shaddai* (God Almighty) in recognition that He had become her Sustainer, Provider, and Redeemer. She needed no other god to supply her need nor did she want any other god than the One in whom she had put her trust and devotion.

Ruth's loyalty to Naomi was not just to a human who meant so much to her, it was to her personal God as well. Therefore, Naomi and her God were inseparable from Ruth. Naomi's people had already become her people when she married Mahlon. To cut those ties would be even more severe than cutting ties with her own family since it involved her personal relationship with Yahweh. To go back to her non-believing home would be unthinkable.

Her statement of faith controlled everything she did and everything she thought. How had she grown so mature? Without belaboring this, it was through the faith and mentoring of Naomi, a person who was so important to her faith that Ruth would have thought it treasonous to go back to her culture and her gods. She couldn't and she wouldn't.

To those of us who were raised in non-Christian homes and then became believers, we know something of what Ruth was stating. When you become a believer, and your family members are not, you become family with those whose ties go deeper than blood. Your church becomes your family. Your spiritual friendships are deeper than you ever imagined. They become your brothers and sisters, your fathers and mothers. You begin to rely on them for spiritual sustenance. I believe we find that kind of relationship between Naomi and Ruth. Naomi was a spiritual mother to Ruth. Those spiritual ties became stronger as time went on. Her commitment was permanent.

Jesus said, "And everyone who has left houses or brothers or sisters or father or mother or children or farms for My name's sake, will receive many times as much, and will inherit eternal life" (Matthew 19:29). Ruth is a clear example of this kind of faith. She had learned well the ways of her teacher. Her faith was in Elohim, maker of heaven and earth and in Yahweh, the great I AM.

Ruth ends her covenant statement with something she could only have learned directly from Naomi. It is the formation of a Jewish covenant that is found several times in the Old Testament. "May the LORD do to me, and worse, if anything but death parts you and me" (Ruth 1:17; 1 Samuel 3:17; 2 Kings 6:31). This was a binding oath that could not be undone. God had become her all in all as seen in her use of the name Yahweh. This oath invoked God's punishment if she didn't follow through on her commitment.

Upon hearing these words, Naomi was speechless. Can a statement like that be met with anything but silence? Ruth would follow up with actions, as we will see in the rest of the story. She understood binding oaths and the consequences from the Lord if she made a statement of loyalty without following through. Naomi would spread the word of Ruth's oath to her friends when she returned home, and these friends would spread the word to others. Eventually, all Israel heard the story about this incredible young woman of faith and her binding covenant to Naomi and Israel's God. Every time the story of Ruth was told, her statement would be repeated.

Ruth, the Friend

In talking about names it is important to also uncover the meaning of Ruth's name, which is "friend." She lived up to that name in every way, first as a life-long friend to Orpah and then as a loyal companion to her precious mother-in-law, Naomi. Here are just a few verses about what it means to be a friend.

- "A friend loves at all times." (Proverbs 17:17)

- "Faithful are the wounds of a friend, but deceitful are the kisses of an enemy." (Proverbs 27:6)

- "Oil and perfume make the heart glad; so a man's counsel is sweet to his friend." (Proverbs 27:9)

- "There is a friend who sticks closer than a brother." (Proverbs 18:24)

- "Greater love has no one than this, that one lay down his life for his friends." (John 15:13)

A friend wants to serve another to make that person's life better. She counsels when necessary and knows when to remain quiet and *just be there*. Friends don't necessarily have to talk and try to figure out or explain what is going on during difficult times. A friend of mine once told me: "Communication takes place face to face, but prayer is when you have the other's back." That's powerful. That's a friend.

What Is a Mentor?

In addition to friendship, the book of Ruth also has much to teach us about mentoring. A mentor is usually a woman who has gone through some of what you are currently facing. She may be in your church, your neighborhood, or may even be a relative. God is gracious in placing people in our lives to mentor or to be mentored by. We will be truly blessed to find such a woman—a second mother—who is older, wiser, and skilled in knowing God. She will influence your life in ways you can't imagine. Listen to her. Watch her. Observe her faith. Follow her as she follows Christ.

If you have never been mentored, I encourage you to ask God to place someone in your life who can lead you and help you where you are most vulnerable. If you are an older woman, know that God is in the business of "placement." He can lead you to young women who need a role model. I have taken on the mantel of this verse, and I urge you to as well: "Older women likewise are to be reverent in their behavior, not malicious gossips nor enslaved to much wine, teaching what is good, so that they may encourage the young women to love their husbands, to love their children" (Titus 2:3-4).

Don and I have had a marriage ministry for most of our married life. We were married in 1967 and suffered through several years of not knowing what to do with marriage. There were no mentors for Don or for me. Then Don got into Scripture and found a track to run on. We began to teach faith-vs.-performance principles to anyone who would listen. We started doing seminars, writing, teaching, and honing our skills. As I look back, I see many men and women who are now walking the faith life in marriage because a young couple struggled and couldn't find help. So, we became that help. We have mentored many, and to God be the glory. We thank Him that He used two strugglers to bring honor to His name.

All of us need to mentor our own children and grandchildren. You must know that you are their best hope of finding faith in God when they are young. But we must also ask God to bring into our children's and grandchildren's lives those who can impact them for eternity. More often it is the parent who does this. Often though, it is another man or woman who is influential in their walk with God. It may be a Sunday school teacher, a youth leader, or a Bible teacher.

God will use many people in our lives to cause us to grow and mature so that we can help others grow and mature. I especially thank God for Young Life leaders who made Christianity so much fun for our kids in their teen years. I thank God for families we hung out with who made an impact in their lives. I thank God for the many who have mentored our children and our grandchildren. Countless lives have been impacted for the kingdom because the role of mentoring was taken seriously.

If you are an older woman, pray about making yourself available to mentor young women. They want to hear how you have come through life experiences. Bible studies are a great place to begin.

God's Placement

The idea of God's placement is also of great importance in the book of Ruth. God took a young couple and *placed* them in a little town in Moab to be the neighbors of two little girls whom He wanted to draw into His Kingdom. Elimelech and Naomi did what God told them to do and because of it we have the world-changing events found in the book of Ruth.

It would have been easy for Naomi to stay in her grief and not get the picture of what God was doing. Likewise, it would have been easy for Ruth to stay in her grief and not go where God was leading her. But neither woman did that. Why? Because they put their faith in a God much bigger than the circumstances of their own lives. They didn't know it at the time but God was not finished writing their stories.

God is not finished writing your story or mine either.

Ruth had quite a testimony already, but it was still unfolding. She had grown up in paganism where child sacrifice, sexual abuse of women, and prostitution were common, all in the name of religion! When Naomi came into her life, Ruth saw something new. Elimelech loved Naomi. There was peace in their home and their sons were wanted and loved. Hard work was an honor. Worshipping Yahweh was filled with wonder.

God rescued Ruth, using Naomi to do so. And now they were on the way to Bethlehem. The journey would have been rough and tiresome. On some days it would have rained, on others the sun would have been scorching. Covering ten miles a day was the maximum pace. Their clothes would be dirty, their hair unkempt, and their feet blistered. They no doubt battled hunger and thirst, but the goal of Bethlehem drove them on.

Questioning God

At this moment both Naomi and Ruth were perplexed with life. Did they ask God why He had taken their husbands? I would have. Hearing His children ask why is not a problem to God. He surely expects it of us. We are not told this in the book, but any mother who loses a child, let alone all the children she has, will undoubtedly ask God *why*. And we know that God may not choose to explain at that point. He may only say, "Trust Me. I love you more than you will ever know. I have a purpose that is not apparent to you right now. I know it hurts. I will get you through." God doesn't waste our trials.

I believe both Naomi and Ruth questioned God. And they would have found that He never rejects our questioning, our petitions, our grieving, our ranting, our tears, our doubts, and even our wrestling. He has His arms open wide to simply hold us to His strong breast. He will wrap His wings around us so we can hover under His strong and loving care.

What kind of God is this? We will unpack this awesome quality of God in the next chapter. But before we go on in this unfolding drama, let's review some key points.

Review

The book of Judges closes with, "In those days there was no king in Israel; everyone did what was right in his own eyes." That book describes a people clamoring for a human king to rule over them. God was to be their one and only King; in this they were to differ from the nations around them. Yet the people argued and rebelled. Against this backdrop God's shines His spotlight on one small family and especially on two women whose only hope is in Him.

These events take place somewhere in the early to middle part of the book of Judges. The pivotal point—the "hinge" if you will—is found in Ruth 1:1 in the meaning of Elimelech's name: *my God is King.*

No matter how bleak the times, God always has a people. They may be small in number, but they are diamonds in the midst of rocks. The book of Ruth is a story about some of these precious few diamonds.

Elimelech and Naomi were walking with God. There is no other reason to call attention to this one small ordinary family. My belief is that had they stayed in Bethlehem, their faith may not have burned as bright. It was in Moab that their faith became real. They were in the center of God's will.

It is now time to bring Ruth to the place where she was to make history: the land of Israel, the territory of Judah, the town of Bethlehem.

Chapter Discussion

1.   Naomi gave a blessing to Ruth and Orpah when she urged them to leave her and return to Moab. Why would she have done this?

2.   Explain the Levirate law of marriage and how it plays into the story of Ruth.

3.   Do you agree or disagree with my thoughts concerning Orpah? Why, or why not?

4.   Within Ruth's covenant statement are two significant commitments. What are they?

5.   Why is it important to follow through on a verbal or written covenant?

6.   Are you presently in a mentoring situation, either mentoring or being mentored?

Chapter 5

Your Trials Matter to God

So they both went until they came to Bethlehem. And when they had come to Bethlehem, that all the city was stirred because of them, and the women said, "Is this Naomi?" She said to them, "Do not call me Naomi; call me Mara, for the Almighty has dealt very bitterly with me. I went out full but the Lord [Yahweh] has brought me back empty. Why do you call me Naomi, since the Lord has witnessed against me and the Almighty [Shaddai] has afflicted me?"

—Ruth 1:19–21

"Don't call me beautiful, call me bitter." What a play on words. Naomi knew she had once been looked upon as beautiful, but at that moment she felt ugly, forgotten, and empty. She was grieving. When bad things happen in a person's life, especially a great loss, grieving is a normal human emotion that God gives us to weather the storm.

Six Stages of Grief

Research on grieving has proven extremely helpful to those who have sustained heavy losses. In her book *On Death and Dying*, psychiatrist Elisabeth Kübler-Ross (5) identified five universal stages of grief. Because I believe grieving *is* addressed by God in His Word, I've added a sixth one (from Scripture) to the descriptions that follow.

1. **Denial**: The shock of loss often produces numbness and an "I can't believe this is happening" into an "I refuse to believe this is happening" response. *Maybe it was a dream*, we may think, *and I will wake up and things will be back to the way they were.*

2. **Anger**: Often the anger is directed at God (*What are you doing to me?!*) or even toward the person who has died (*Why did you leave me?*).

3. **Bargaining**: This is when we wrestle with the what-ifs, as in: *What if he hadn't gone to work that day? What if the doctor had done such and such? What if I had been there?* and so on. These questions haunt us because the answers are unknowable and there are no guarantees that the outcome would have been different.

4. **Depression**: This heaviness sets in when we begin to realize there is nothing we or anyone else can do to change the situation. Depression is often accompanied by sleeplessness, exhaustion, and feeling as if we'd rather die than live.

5. **Acceptance**: We come to a general acceptance of our new life when our thoughts include such attitudes as: *This is my life now. Life goes on. I can go on. I will go on. Life will be different, but I will live and move into the future.*

6. **Praise and thanksgiving**: As we embrace the sovereignty of God through our loss, He will enable us with a thankful heart of worship. This may be the most important stage of grieving. God doesn't say to be thankful *for* the loss but to give thanks *in* all things (see 1 Thessalonians 5:17).

All of these stages are important to our wrestling with God. They may not necessarily come in this order, and we may even go back and forth between them, sometimes at a deeper level than before. It is also helpful for us to keep in mind that trials generally take longer than we expect.

In my thinking, Naomi was probably somewhere between the third and fourth stage, that is between anger and depression. Remember, she described herself as *bitter*. She adeptly defined what she was going through. She was open and honest and did not try to hide the bitterness of soul that had drained the beauty of her countenance.

She was not the same person her friends knew when she was younger. Then she had been full of hope, life, and vision for the future. Now she was numb from the heavy toll of her losses. Her hopes and dreams had been shattered. Pain was etched into her face and her words were bitter. Life had passed her by. She had nothing to look forward to.

My friend, Dixie Fraley Keller, in her *Widow's Workbook* (6) said this. "Grieving will come over you like a pall. It will seem to suffocate you. One of the first responses, in fact, is an apparent lack of breath. It feels as if the breath of life has departed from you as well as from your loved one. . . . You will feel overwhelmed because you are overwhelmed. The shock of death can be overpowering. The flood of emotions can be devastating, exhausting you to the core of your being."

We must also remember that Naomi and Ruth had traveled a very long distance. They were no doubt sore, aching, disheveled, exhausted, and dirty. They were probably parched, hungry and very much in need of a bath. Of course Naomi didn't look the same! Who would have?

At this point it may be helpful to keep in mind what our response should be when a person has gone through tragedy or loss of any kind, for the most part, words complicate things. This is why it is generally better to simply say, "I don't begin to understand what you have been through, but I want you to know I am here for you. If you need to talk, I am here. If you need me to sit with you, I am here". Often we try to make sense of the situation and only make things worse. Don't confuse the issue with remarks that offend like, just "Trust the Lord," or "The Lord knows what He is doing."

Again Dixie Keller said, "Please give your widowed friends room to grieve in the way that best facilitates their grieving process, even if it differs from the way you process grief. Give yourself room to process your own grief. . . Allow yourself and those around you the space to breathe and adjust. . . . Grieving is not just about you. You are not an island in this process (even though you may feel that way). Loss impacted me personally but it impacted so many others too." (4)

El Shaddai Revealed

God reveals Himself through His names throughout Scripture. In the book of Ruth, God is going to re-introduce His people to another of His names: El Shaddai, or Almighty. Incidentally, this is one of my favorite names of God. This name was a very personal and warm way to refer to God in the Old Testament. The fuller meaning is "the all sufficient One, the Provider, *the Strong-Breasted One.*"

Even in her admitted state of bitterness, Naomi acknowledged that through all of her trials she had been under El Shaddai. Naomi believed in the sovereignty of God, though she didn't always like the finality of it. She didn't understand His dealings with her, yet she leaned on Him. She knew God was her only hope, her only provision. And that's why she called Him El Shaddai.

God was Naomi's strength in weakness. It was to Him she carried her pain. He had been her sustainer in times of famine and now in a time of sorrow. And unknown to her, through Ruth, He would sustain and provide for her even more than she could imagine.

Yet for a while Naomi would continue to grieve, as we all find ourselves doing at one time or another in life. And we find, as Naomi surely did, that grieving is right and necessary. We are meant to understand that down the road there will be light at the end of the dark tunnel. God doesn't want us to get stuck. He will move us through our grieving as we follow Him. Psalm 56:8 says, "Put my tears in Your bottle. are they not in Your book?" God takes note of our tears; they are precious to Him. In Revelation 7:17 we read that one day God will wipe away every tear. How wonderful! And Revelation 21:4 assures us that when that day comes, there will no longer be any mourning, or crying, or pain. This is our hope as we go through our fallen world. One day . . .

It was good that in her grieving Naomi recognized the sovereignty of God at work in her life. Perhaps there was hope for new joy. In the meantime she turned to the familiar to help her in her journey. She needed her old friends and family, even though they didn't understand all she had been through. El Shaddai was directing her steps. He was leading her forward.

I do find it interesting that Naomi told the women that she left full but came back empty, with Ruth standing right next to her. Did this statement hurt

Ruth? If so, she didn't let on. She said nothing in her own defense. Of course, we understand that Naomi had left with a husband and two sons and had returned without them, but Ruth had recently made an unbelievable promise—a covenant—to her, and here was Naomi saying to her friends that she had come back empty. I think I would have cleared my throat, loudly, to remind my mother-in-law that I was standing next to her!

El Shaddai would help Naomi to fully appreciate what He had given to her, but it would take time and observation.

Job

I like to think of Naomi in terms of Job and his wife. Job seemed to pass the test of loss so much better than most of us can even imagine. But I identify more with Mrs. Job. Let me recap some of the story.

> There was a man in the land of Uz whose name was Job; and that man was blameless, upright, fearing God and turning away from evil. Seven sons and three daughters were born to him. (Job 1:1–2)

Job had great possessions and wealth. Satan asked permission from God to test Job's faith by taking these things away. Next, Satan asked God to take away all Job's servants by the hands of the Chaldeans. Eventually, Satan is allowed to broaden his attack to the deaths of Job's ten children and to his physical health. When they (remember, they were a couple) lost material possessions, I am sure Mrs. Job took it the best she could. But when she lost her ten children . . . Oh my, my mind reels with that loss! (See Job 1:13–22)

Job seems to have kept perspective on who God was and what material possessions meant in light of his relationship with the Almighty. Job's wife, however, momentarily lost sight of who God was. I can understand that. Have you ever been in such pain that you felt you lost sight of God? All loss brings pain, but the sudden death of *all* your children? She had carried them in her womb. She had nursed them at her breast. She had laughed and cried with each precious child. Could faith possibly lift Mrs. Job's heart from their graves?

> Then his wife said to him, "Do you still hold fast your integrity? Curse God and die!" But he said to her, "You speak as one of the foolish women speaks. Shall we indeed accept good from God and not accept adversity?" In all this Job did not sin with his lips. (Job 2:9–10)

Though his words may sound harsh, I believe Job was actually being kind to his wife in stating what he did. He was trying to cause her to look beyond her circumstances and loss to who God was. But as a woman, I can understand Mrs. Job's despair. I have eleven grandchildren. I cannot fathom losing every one of them in a single day. My material possessions are not flesh and blood. They can come and go. But my children and grandchildren are a whole different story. Mrs. Job knew God had been the One who took her children. She looked at Job and said, "Just curse God and die." Honestly, I think I might have said the same thing. She was below empty. She was in the deepest, darkest tunnel imaginable.

In my opinion, people are way too hard on Mrs. Job. She was a woman who loved her children more than her own life. When those precious souls were taken from her, well . . . words are insufficient. And it seems that God was *not* hard on her. At the end of the book of Job, where God expressed his great displeasure with Job's friends for badly misrepresenting Him, and demanded a sacrifice for their repentance, we see no such rebuke directed at her. He understood her pain and anguish. He understood her words, her lament, her doubting at His goodness. He understood her wrestling with Him and loved her for it. He simply drew her under His almighty wings.

Instead, "God blessed the latter days of Job [and Mrs. Job] more than his beginning" (Job 42:12). God gave back, not only to him, but to her as well. They had ten more children and lived a full life after that, raising their children, having a relationship with their grandchildren and great grandchildren (Job 42:13–17). God did indeed take away, but He also gave!

God made women. He loves us unconditionally, and He understands our hearts when it comes to our children and grandchildren. He made us to nurture and care for them. We know they are His from the beginning, and we are so thankful when He gives us children to raise. The pain is unbearable when any one of them is taken.

Mrs. Job and Naomi would have understood each other well. They both knew that God is El Shaddai, a name of God they learned in the darkness of grief. Wings of comfort hover over the souls of broken faith.

Our Year of Trials

Have you ever been in a place where you didn't understand what on earth God was doing in your life? Perhaps you experienced a broken engagement, divorce, the death of a loved one, or you were fired from your job, went through bankruptcy, were deeply hurt by a friend or family member, or were caught up in a church split. You knew God was God and He *could* have prevented what happened. And you probably asked Him why He didn't.

When we are in a period of trial, we don't have the perspective of history on our side. We are making history, not understanding it. Often, when we are in a trial, we look at other people instead of God. We ask questions. We feel like a failure. We feel like God is turning a deaf ear to our cries. What does faith look like in those moments? Is it visible or is it tucked under the brokenness of life?

In 2011-2012 our family went through a series of trials. Our youngest daughter, age thirty-six and the mother of three young children, had her yearly check-up. Her doctor wanted her to begin having mammograms for a baseline. Three days later she was told that she had breast cancer. She needed to have a double mastectomy immediately.

Two weeks after her diagnosis, our oldest daughter, age forty-one, was diagnosed with the identical breast cancer. She, too, is the mother of three young children. Both of my daughters went through double mastectomies and reconstruction within the year.

What a tough year. Did I wrestle with God? You bet I did! I asked all the questions others ask. Questions that had no answers.

Email to My Friends
October 17, 2011

Our news isn't good tonight. Many of you know that two weeks ago Tiffany (age 36) was diagnosed with breast cancer and will undergo a double mastectomy. Today we found out that Carmen (age 41) was diagnosed with the identical cancer and will undergo a double mastectomy within a month or two at the most.

We know all things work together for good to those who love the Lord, so we are standing on that promise. We know God's heart and that His heart is good.

I have thought of the story of the man born blind and Jesus was asked who sinned, this man or his parents. In other words, whose fault is this? (John 9:1–3) Of course I struggled with what *I* did to cause my daughters to get cancer. What did I feed them when young? What chemicals did I expose them to? What did I do?

To the question of the blind man, Jesus replied, "It was neither that this man sinned, nor his parents; but it was so that the works of God might be displayed in him."

We believe that God's glory will shine through our trials. Is cancer scary? Yes. But God tells us not to fear.

Our other daughter, Kathryn, had a baby five months ago and is breast-feeding. She is going to begin the process of stopping so that in three months she, too, will have her first mammogram and be tested for cancer as well.

We do not have breast cancer in the family that we know of, so what is causing this? We don't know, but maybe the Lord will let us find some answers as to why breast cancer is so prevalent.

My heart has certainly been heavy. Tears have come and gone for all of us, but we go through this as a strong, close family, each one being the other's best friend—and, of course, the Lord who is our entire family's best friend.

Tiffany's Facebook Entry

November 10, 2011, the day before her surgery

This morning I ran my last run before surgery tomorrow. A very reflective run it was. As I ran I couldn't help but think about this course I'm signed up to run starting tomorrow that I know nothing about. Everyone's versions of the course are different and unique, as will be mine. But, somewhere in the 5th mile I was reminded of a conversation I had over the summer regarding my daughter Kate (9). As many of you know, we've been on quite a journey with her in the past 10 years. We've seen more specialists, doctors, therapists, etc., than I'd like to recall. But over the summer we decided to embark on one last ditch effort to come up with a written diagnosis for her school and teachers. We had a very highly recommended team of specialists and doctors do an in depth evaluation of her intellectually, emotionally and neurologically. At the end of the two months, a representative of the team looked at me and said, "I'm sorry. I know you've paid a lot of money but your child is the most unique, perplexing, and fascinating child we've seen in 25 years. We just don't have a diagnosis. She just doesn't fit in any perfectly square box." To which I replied, "Thank you, that's the best news I've gotten in 10 years." He looked at me confused and I said, "Isn't that the way we should see our children? Unique and fascinating. Furthermore, isn't that the way we should see life? There are always things that come that don't fit in the perfectly square box we've created.

Fast forward to October 3, 2011. The doctor says, "I'm sorry but you have cancer." To which I replied, "OK, this will be quite a journey but I've already learned that life doesn't fit in a perfectly square box. God never promised it would. He did promise to get me through it."

So, here it is people: I learned a long time ago that it's really not about me. That my strength and my endurance always eventually fail. But, God's strength becomes resilience. God's endurance produces character and God's peace is eternal. I know I'm not the only one looking up at a hill and wondering how high it goes. But, if we only focus on the hill, we will miss the blessing on the other side.

Thank you for all of your prayers! I will never be able to thank all of you for your emails, text messages, calls, meals, gifts, and prayers. But, please know that I am so completely thankful for each one of you!!!

Carmen's Post to Her Friends
Surgery was scheduled for Feb. 4, 2012

Hello Friends!

I just wanted to take the time to say thank you so much to each and every one of you for your support and prayers for me during this time! It truly means the world to me! I feel so comforted and peaceful knowing there are so many people lifting me up in prayer. This is not a road I would have chosen, but now that I am on it, I can see the blessings from it. This is one of those blessings—people coming together in the body of Christ to pray. God and the angels must rejoice at something like this! How neat! So thank you for your prayers!

I am truly at peace tonight. It is amazing to me. God is so good. Please continue to pray that there is no infection. The infection risk continues for several weeks after surgery as long as the drains are in which can be 4-6 weeks. Obviously we are praying that the cancer has not spread and there is no cancer in the lymph nodes. Hope all this helps with how to pray specifically.

We will never know this side of heaven the impact that your prayers have. I can't wait to get to heaven and ask God about this time in my life and what was going on in the spiritual world around me. How each and every one of your prayers helped me bit by bit get through this. I think it will blow me away! We have so much to look forward to learning! My prayer would be that God receives all the glory and honor for this whole situation, that this would truly be about Him and not about me.

With much love and gratitude, and a very humbled heart, Carmen

Prayers of the Saints

Hundreds of emails and notes were sent from faithful friends who carried the banner of prayer for these precious girls. My faith was tested, Tiffany's and Carmen's faith was tested, their husbands' faith was tested. I watched as my precious daughters leaned heavily on the Lord. They have such simple faith and went through all of it with grace and, yes, joy. Their hearts were flooded with peace as they faced the future knowing God was in control.

Below is a song that ministered greatly to me during our times of testing: I played and sang it often. These are very special words.

Blessings by Laura Story (7))

We pray for blessings
We pray for peace
Comfort for family, protection while we sleep
We pray for healing, for prosperity
We pray for Your mighty hand to ease our suffering
All the while, You hear each spoken need
Yet love us way too much to give us lesser things

'Cause what if Your blessings come through raindrops
What if Your healing comes through tears
What if a thousand sleepless nights
Are what it takes to know You're near
What if trials of this life are Your mercies in disguise

We pray for wisdom Your voice to hear
And we cry in anger when we cannot feel You near
We doubt Your goodness, we doubt Your love
As if every promise from Your Word is not enough
All the while, You hear each desperate plea
And long that we have faith to believe

'Cause what if Your blessings come through raindrops
What if Your healing comes through tears
What if a thousand sleepless nights
Are what it takes to know You're near
And what if trials of this life are Your mercies in disguise

When friends betray us
When darkness seems to win
We know that pain reminds this heart
That this is not, this is not our home
It's not our home

Cause what if Your blessings come through raindrops
What if Your healing comes through tears
And what if a thousand sleepless nights
Are what it takes to know You're near
What if my greatest disappointments
Or the achings of this life
Is the revealing of a greater thirst this world can't satisfy
And what if trials of this life
The rain, the storms, the hardest nights
Are Your mercies in disguise.

⁓

More Trials

I'm not finished with that year yet! At age 72, I fell twice and injured my back. Don, also at age 72, fell and dislocated his shoulder. One grandson had ear surgery after falling off a trampoline. And two daughters, Carmen and Kathryn, each had a car accident and totaled their cars. So that year was painful for me as a mom and grandmother. And, yes, I wrestled with God.

God kept hammering this verse into my head as I lay before Him once again my dear daughters: "Consider it all joy, my brethren, when you encounter various trials . . ." (James 1:2). I had given my children to

Him at their births. He had tested me over the years, but none like this one—the "C" word. We had encountered cancer before, first with Don's prostate cancer and then with Kathryn's melanoma. Both had surgery and remained cancer free. Until recently. While writing this book, we learned that Don had cancer of the kidney. Upon hearing the news, we looked at each other and simply said, "Well, it's another bridge to cross and we will cross it." Thankfully, the cancer was detected early and was able to be frozen.

In addition to four of our family members having dealt with cancer, two of our children went through years of infertility issues. Todd and Sara and Brandon and Kathryn were each married seven years and both couples went through in vitro fertilization—a painful, time consuming, expensive process. Numerous eggs were fertilized with most of them failing to mature. Disappointment after disappointment. Sara went through the whole process twice, and God eventually gave them three wonderful daughters.

Kathryn's first in vitro pregnancy ended in miscarriage. The second time around she got pregnant with her first son. This was followed by further disappointment when no other eggs matured. They thought they were finished, but then they got pregnant naturally with a sweet little girl.

We may try to prepare for trials, but I have found they come when we are least expecting them and in ways we can't predict. God doesn't give us warning. He does promise to go through the trials with us, hovering over us as a mother bird hovers over her chicks. What comfort. What love. What peace during troublesome days. My children have often told me they have simple faith. It was never more evident than during those dark days when questions came and answers did not.

Trials on Every Page, in Every Life

No one is exempt from trials. The pages of Scripture carry the stories of men and women who, though following Him, went through a trial or series of trials.

- Adam and Eve's second son was murdered at the hand of their firstborn.
- Noah faced the death of everyone he knew, except his immediate family.
- Job and Mrs. Job lost all their children on one tragic day.
- Abraham was asked by God to sacrifice his only son.
- Jacob lived for years in fear of a brother who hated him.
- Leah longed to be loved by her husband, Jacob.
- Joseph was betrayed by his own brothers and then put in prison for something he didn't do.
- Moses questioned his ability and competence, even though God had called him.
- David's loyalty was met with hatred.
- Esther was forced to put her very life on the line.
- Paul was put in prison for his faith.
- Every disciple was murdered for his faith, except John.

Why do we think God is doing something different in our lives than He did in every person who has ever trusted Him as Savior and Lord? God is doing something, not so unique in outcome, as unique in trials. In other words, the trial may be different, but the outcome results in dependence and trust in El Shaddai.

We cannot understand the ways of God. Trust and obedience are required of us in the darkest places of our lives, even when understanding seems impossible.

Ancient Memory

Within each of us is an "ancient memory," causing us to realize that things aren't supposed to be the way they are now. When the world was new, it was perfect. There was no pain, no trials, no disappointments. Life was good and whole (Genesis 1–2). Then sin became a reality for our first parents and for all generations that would follow. We live in a fallen world (Genesis 3). When we experience pain and brokenness and loss we know this isn't what it was meant to be. The invisible war continues unabated throughout our lives. We live *on* the battlefield. One of my friends, Jerry Phillips, once said, "I'm still in the battle and it's bloody out here." Isn't that how we would portray our lives? We don't like this present darkness. We want light. We want life.

But deep within us we also have a future hope that someday life will be whole again. We look forward to all that God promised; God has set eternity in our hearts (Ecclesiastes 3:11). Praise God, we don't have to live forever in such a fallen state. There is a new world coming where all will be right (Revelation 21–22). But not yet. . . . .

Chapter Discussion

1. Have you gone through any of the stages of grief? Share your story.

2. Describe how wrestling with God can be beneficial.

3. Describe the importance of the name of God, El Shaddai.

4. What are your thoughts about Mrs. Job?

5. What ministered most to you during your last trial?

Chapter 6

There Are No Accidents with God

So Naomi returned, and with her Ruth the Moabitess, her daughter-in-law, who returned from the land of Moab. And they came to Bethlehem at the beginning of barley harvest.

Now Naomi had a kinsman of her husband, a man of great wealth, of the family of Elimelech, whose name was Boaz. And Ruth the Moabitess said to Naomi, "Please let me go to the field and glean among the ears of grain after one in whose sight I may find favor." And she said to her, "Go, my daughter." So she departed and went and gleaned in the field after the reapers; and she happened to come to the portion of the field belonging to Boaz, who was of the family of Elimelech.

—Ruth 1:22, 2:1–3

Notice the word *happened* in Ruth 2:3, and let's consider the "happenstance" of God. Thus far in the book of Ruth we've seen Elimelech and Naomi *happen* to sojourn into Moab to the very village of Ruth. Then we saw Ruth *happen* to marry Mahlon who *happened* to die before he and Ruth had children. Now we have the widowed Ruth and her widowed mother-in-law, Naomi, *happening* to return to Bethlehem—the "house of bread"—at harvest time. Furthermore, when Ruth goes to glean in the fields so that she and Naomi could eat, she *happened* to come into the property of Boaz who *happened* to be a relative.

Large families often owned adjoining farmland. This was probably the case here. Elimelech's property would have likely remained fallow from the time of his departure for Moab. Boaz was a wealthy relative whose fields Ruth had entered.

You and I know that what looks like happenstance is, in reality, the sovereignty of God at work. I believe the essence of the book of Ruth is the providence and provision of El Shaddai. On every page, at every turn, we see the hand of God directing the steps of this godly family. And now He has brought Boaz into the story.

Happenstance or Placement?

Consider "happenstance" in your life. Was your birth just a random happening? What about your family lineage? Do those people play any significant role in shaping the person you are or are they just . . . people? And your spouse, did the two of you just happen to meet or did God bring you together?

Do you agree that God's fingerprints are all over your life, from beginning to end? He not only determined who your parents would be and when you would be born, but He has also determined when you will die and all the events and circumstances in between. For example:

He chose us in Him before the foundation of the world. (Ephesians 1:4)

Since his days are determined, the number of his months is with You; and his limits You have set so that he cannot pass. (Job 14:5)

Your eyes have seen my unformed substance; and in Your book were all written the days that were ordained for me, when as yet there was not one of them. (Psalm 139:16)

He made from one man every nation of mankind to live on all the face of the earth, having determined their appointed times and the boundaries of their habitation, that they would seek God, if perhaps they might grope for Him and find Him, though He is not far from each one of us; for in Him we live and move and exist. (Acts 17:26–28)

These passages indicate that God has determined our lives before we were conceived. Scripture also says that God has numbered our days, our hours, our moments on this earth—a number we cannot go beyond no matter what we eat, how much we exercise, or how we live. Our quantity of life is preset. Maybe by eating right and exercising we can affect the quality of our life, but just as we didn't control our birth, we cannot control our death or the circumstances that will bring it about.

Just so, Naomi could not have prevented her husband's and sons' deaths. She was not in control, God was. If she could have done anything to prevent their deaths, she would have. She realized how powerless and humbling death can be. Yet God still had much of life to show her. There were joys to come that she could not imagine now. Her adventure with Him was not over. She would come to understand more clearly God's sovereignty in her life and in the life of her dear daughter-in-law. And she would like the next few chapters yet to be revealed. But for now she was in deep sorrow and bewilderment.

Accidents

You will not find the word *accident* in your Bible's concordance. Go ahead, look it up. Accident is not a word penned by the Holy Spirit. From our point of view, we may experience accidents, but God is never surprised by the turn of events in our lives. Each turn has a purpose. Our responsibility is to trust Him at those turns, understanding that He knows what's best for us in the long run. We may hurt at any given change, but God is doing something that we never could have planned ourselves. He sees the beginning from the end and all the twists and turns in between. He knows what He is doing in our lives although to us it may seem a mystery.

"I am the Lord, and there is no other;besides Me there is no God. I will gird you, though you have not known Me. That men may know from the rising to the setting of the sun that there is no one besides Me. I am the Lord, and there is no other.

The One forming light and creating darkness, causing well-being and creating calamity; I am the Lord who does all these.' (Isaiah 45:5-7)

"For My thoughts are not your thoughts, nor are your ways My ways," declares the Lord.

"For as the heavens are higher than the earth, so are My ways higher than your ways and My thoughts than your thoughts." (Isaiah 55:8-9)

There is neither happenstance nor accidents with God, for He sees the future as clearly as He sees the past. Ours is to trust Him, even though we may have doubts and questions.

The Law of Gleaning

God had made it clear that there were to be no hungry people in the land. Poor yes, hungry no (Matthew 26:11). One way that hunger was to be addressed was through the law of gleaning.

If you were a landowner, you were commanded not to harvest the whole crop. You were to leave some for the needy, whether widows, strangers, orphaned, or jobless. This was a welfare system of sorts in which recipients were required to work in order to eat.

Gleaning was hard fieldwork; it required following after the reapers and harvesting the crops they had left standing or picking up the pieces that had fallen by the wayside. According to the law, the reapers were not to harvest the corners of the fields so more grain would be available for the gleaners.

Now when you reap the harvest of your land, you shall not reap to the very corners of your field, nor shall you gather the gleanings of your harvest. Nor shall you glean your vineyard, nor shall you gather the fallen fruit of your vineyard; you shall leave them for the needy and for the stranger. For I am the LORD your God. (Leviticus 19:9–10)

The reason behind the law of gleaning is given in Deuteronomy 24:22: "You shall remember that you were a slave in the land of Egypt." In other words, the people were to remember their own days of hunger and poverty, and through their empathy, reach out to the poor. God would bless them for it. The widow, orphan, and stranger did not have means of support, so God's people were to become their means.

Naomi would have explained the law of gleaning to Ruth, perhaps while on their journey from Moab to Bethlehem. In the case of widows, if you were a young widow it was generally assumed that you would remarry and your husband would be your provider. If you did not remarry, or until you did, the laws of the Old Testament instructed how to provide for yourself and your family. If you were older, your kinsmen—brothers, sons, cousins, and the like—were responsible for your welfare.

Incidentally, this is still the case in many parts of the world and was generally true in the United States until about 1950 when our society began looking more to the government and away from the family. Notice a contrast here between what God put in place for provision and what our country has done in the last one hundred years. Families were always responsible to take care of each other. There were no government programs such as Medicare, Medicaid, food stamps, social security, pensions, senior citizens homes, and assisted living. The government cannot adequately do what families have always done. Governments don't love, people do.

God's Provision

God provides for us through others, and He provides for others through us (employment, wages, gifts, and charity). God has ordained work. Work is good for us, and it is our responsibility. Through work God provides. Ruth, in gleaning, would provide for herself and Naomi. This is one more demonstration of these ladies' trust in El Shaddai, observing the law of gleaning—as both a right and a responsibility—to gain provision. El Shaddai brought them under His protective wing and led them to the right portion of land from which to glean, the fields of Boaz.

Chapter Discussion

1.   In what ways can we see the sovereignty of God at work in the circumstances of Naomi and Ruth?

2.   Describe a circumstance or event in your life that, though it may have seemed like "happenstance," was really the sovereignty of God.

3.   Explain the differences between the welfare system of Old Testament Israel and modern-day US.

4.   Why is it important for us to understand and acknowledge how God provides for us?

5.   Why was training in obedience good for Israel as a nation?

6.   How does God train us in obedience?

Chapter 7

Your Work Matters to God

Just as one set of parents named their son Elimelech, or *our God is King*, another set of parents named their son Boaz, or *in Him is strength*. Both of these men, and their names, stand out as bookends in the story of Ruth.

Remember that during the three-hundred-year period when judges ruled the nation Israel, the people did what was right in their own eyes and rebelled against God. They wanted to be like the surrounding nations, so they demanded that God appoint a king to rule over them. Still, there was a faithful remnant who believed that God alone should be their king. Within that remnant was a family from the tribe of Judah. Within that family were two men: Elimelech and Boaz.

Boaz the Employer

> Now behold, Boaz came from Bethlehem and said to the reapers, "May the LORD be with you." And they said to him, "May the LORD bless you." (Ruth 2:4)

Boaz was a godly man who treated his employees with respect, even to the point of blessing them at the start of the workday. Blessings were common among families, but not so common from an employer to his subordinates. Boaz must have been a man who stood out in a crowd. One didn't pronounce blessings on his workers if he was mean-spirited and selfish, which wealthy landowners often were. Blessings come from the heart of a man who is kind and generous.

The way his employees responded also tells a lot about Boaz. They reciprocated with a blessing of their own: "May the LORD bless you." Both the employer and the employees bless one another and in doing so bless the Lord. You can almost feel the kindness of God in this man and his actions. Clearly he was a man of integrity who had earned the respect and loyalty of his workers.

I believe Boaz's employees worked hard for him because he was a man of his word who treated them fairly. He probably knew most of their families and any struggles they may have been going through. Boaz didn't seek wealth, power, or fame, although God had blessed him with those things. He was simply serving God in the place where God had placed him.

Healthy Relationships: marriage, family and work

Ephesians chapters 5 and 6 address numerous types of relationships and how God desires for them to work. The lead-in of this passage on relationships is Ephesians 5:21: "Submit to one another out of reverence for Christ" (NIV). The passage then defines the roles of husband/wife, fathers/children, and employers/employees. Let's particularly look at this passage in light of the life and character of Boaz.

> Slaves [employees], be obedient to those who are your masters [employers] according to the flesh, with fear and trembling, in the sincerity of your heart, as to Christ; not by way of eyeservice, as men-pleasers, but as slaves of Christ, doing the will of God from the heart. With good will render service, as to the Lord, and not to men, knowing that whatever good thing each one does, this he will receive back from the Lord, whether slave or free.
>
> And masters [employers], do the same things to them, and give up threatening, knowing that both their Master and yours is in heaven, and there is no partiality with Him. (Ephesians 6:5–9)

Submitting to one another requires that we *listen* to one another, that we pay attention to not only the words spoken but also to the heart behind them. We should show grace in the way we communicate, whether listening or responding. This level of communication causes us to recognize one another as image-bearers of God and is an expression of submitting to one another with reverence for Christ. I submit to you while you are talking by listening, hearing your heart, and responding appropriately. When I am the talker and you are the listener, you submit to me in the same fashion.

Think of this in terms of the various relationships addressed in Ephesians 5. If a married couple has had a disagreement, the wife will feel loved when her husband submits to her by listening to her heart and acknowledging that he heard her and will do what he can to make things right. He may not be able to fix everything, but she needs to know that he has heard her. On the other hand, she will likely become angrier if she has not been heard; this is a reaction to being devalued as an image bearer of God. In the same way, the husband feels respected when his wife listens to him, acknowledges that she hears him, and values him. But he, too, will react to being devalued or unduly ignored or criticized.

Similarly, in the parent-child relationship, a dad or mom can exasperate their children by not communicating through both words and heart. If a parent stops to listen to their child, the child feels valued as an image-bearer of God. Some parents demand obedience through harsh words and tone, which generally results in anger and defiance—the opposite of what the parent hoped for. In addition to behavioral problems, the relationship itself is broken.

Finally, think of employer and employee. An employee feels valued, and even loved, when his employer listens—again, to words and heart. Conversely, that same employer will create feelings of resentment and anger by use of threatening speech and harsh words, or by simply not listening to and valuing the opinions of his workers. When an employee has an issue with the company or business, he is often afraid of discussing the matter with his boss. The employer needs to make it safe for people to air grievances, share concerns, or offer ideas. If such safety does not exist, employees will get discouraged, perhaps stir up feelings of disloyalty among other workers, or just leave. Both parties suffer.

Ephesians 5 and 6 can be applied to any relationship where there are two people and one has authority over the other. The one in authority has to create a safe environment for healthy communication. Christ said that the greatest commandment is to love the Lord your God with all you heart, mind, and strength. The second commandment is to love your neighbor as yourself (Luke 10:27). Loving means being able to give of yourself (submitting yourself) to another so the other person feels loved and cared for.

Boaz: An Example of Christ

Ruth felt honored and cared for by Boaz from the moment she stepped into his fields. How? He engaged her in conversation, and then listened to what she had to say. As we unpack the rest of the passage we will learn more about his Christ-like treatment of employees, the needy, and strangers. He was a clear and living example of Ephesians 5:21.

Boaz epitomized his name: the strength of the Lord was his banner, and his relationship with God was key to his relationships with others. Almost every time he speaks, his words take the form of a blessing, an encouragement, or the reassurance of safety. He talked openly of the Lord and His ways.

Boaz ate and fellowshipped with his employees, not thinking he was above them in any respect. His workplace was pleasant, with refreshment breaks and all. His employees didn't want to work anywhere else. Nor did Boaz treat the poor gleaners any differently than his paid workers. Both were able to sit at the same table. I gain from his character that he treated each one with dignity, as image bearers of God, not based on what they could do for him. So often in the workplace employers don't listen to those most loyal to them. They treat some with great respect who make them look good, yet others are not treated with respect. Some employers criticize without also complimenting. (The same can also be said of husbands/wives and fathers/children.)

Listen in on one of Boaz's conversations. Notice his awareness of his employees. Watch his protection of his workers. Listen to his authority.

Boaz asked the overseer of his harvesters, "Who does that young woman belong to?" [Who is her husband or father?] The overseer replied, "She is the Moabite, who came back from Moab with Naomi. She said, 'Please let me glean and gather among the sheaves behind the harvesters.' She came into the field and has remained here from morning till now, except for a short rest in the shelter."

So Boaz said to Ruth, "My daughter, listen to me. Don't go and glean in another field and don't go away from here. Stay here with the women who work for me. Watch the field where the men are harvesting, and follow along after the women. I have told the men not to lay a hand on you. And whenever you are thirsty, go and get a drink from the water jars the men have filled." (Ruth 2:5–9, NIV)

Because Boaz lived in a time of great apostasy in Israel, where men followed hard after their lusts, he wanted to protect this young woman from any harm that might befall her. Before he approached Ruth, he went to his male employees and commanded them not to touch her in any way. That command carried the threat of punishment if they misbehaved. He was strong. He was authoritative. He was firm.

Boaz saw in Ruth a woman whose heart was good. And, he saw her vulnerability. He had respect for her simply because she was a woman. Godly men respect women. They do not want to use them for their own selfish pleasure. Rather, they see beauty that must be cared for. They see the feminine expression of the image of God (Genesis 1:27). To violate her in any way would be an affront to God Himself. Boaz would not let that happen.

Ruth was overwhelmed with his protective nature. Boaz called her "my daughter" because of her age. She was young, he was old. He did not see in her, nor did she see in him, anything that would have led to a closer relationship. She was a gleaner, he a wealthy landowner. That was all. He was simply going to provide for her. His character showed through in everything he said and did. He hired workers, he provided for gleaners. He was careful to oversee and protect all who came under his charge and he did it with grace and care.

At this, she bowed down with her face to the ground. She asked him, "Why have I found such favor in your eyes that you notice me—a foreigner?"

Boaz replied, "I've been told all about what you have done for your mother-in-law since the death of your husband—how you left your father and mother and your homeland and came to live with a people you did not know before. May the LORD repay you for what you have done. May you be richly rewarded by the LORD, the God of Israel, under whose wings you have come to seek refuge." (Ruth 2:10–12, NIV)

El Shaddai: The Strong-Breasted One

This is the second high point in the book of Ruth. The first was Ruth's statement of loyalty to Naomi (1:16–17), and now this statement is made in the form of a blessing from Boaz to Ruth. It will carry incredible meaning for a future that is, for the time being, unknown to either one of them. Pay special attention to the words "under whose wings you have come to seek refuge" in verse 12. This is a picture of El Shaddai, and calls to mind the image of Jesus taking such loving and protective care of his bride (the church) that He pulls her under his wings.

Boaz may have known of Naomi before she and Elimelech left for Moab. He possibly knew of her family as they were related through marriage and all lived in Bethlehem. However, theirs was a large tribe so they may not have had a great deal of interaction. Boaz was a close relative of Elimelech, so they must have known each other fairly well. They grew up in the same town, went to the same synagogue, and may have been close in age. They also owned land in the same proximity.

How did Boaz know of Ruth, though? Obviously, through Naomi. Upon returning to Bethlehem, Naomi would have told her people about the years in Moab, about meeting Ruth and her family, about meeting Orpah and her family, about the marriages of her sons, and the deaths of her husband and sons. She no doubt would have described Ruth's commitment and her refusal to return to her family and culture.

Naomi must have also told of Ruth's willingness to glean in the hot sun in order to provide for her. Ruth's reputation of goodness and loyalty to her mother-in-law had become known. And news of it had reached Boaz.

Boaz: A Man of Blessings

Boaz, as we've already noticed, was in the habit of pronouncing blessings on people. He gave blessings to those who worked for him, and now he gives a blessing to a widow in need. His blessing to Ruth included: (1) a prayer that God would reward her work, (2) the hope that her wages from the Lord would be full, and (3) the recognition that she had sought refuge in the right place— under the wings of El Shaddai.

Almost immediately God began to fulfill this blessing through Boaz himself. When he told Ruth not to glean in anyone else's field, has was offering her protection, putting her under his wings. God often uses people to fulfill our needs, our prayers, and our provisions. But we must remember that it is always El Shaddai who ultimately fulfills them.

The Genealogy of a Psalmist

Boaz's great grandson, David, uses the imagery of God placing us under His wings seven times in the psalms he wrote. Why was this phrase so often on David's mind? Could it be that this description of God was special in David's ancestry, having been taught to him by his father, Jesse, who had been taught by his father, Obed, who had learned it from his father, Boaz? Interesting.

I believe that David was the author of the book of Ruth. It is after all, a book about his great grandparents. Their story would have been passed down to him through his tribal ancestry. Who better to write it than their great grandson, the poet and psalmist?

Notice the similarity of what Boaz said to Ruth—"under whose wings you have come to seek refuge"(2:12)—to the phraseology of David.

- Hide me in the shadow of your wings. (Psalm 17:8)
- The children of men take refuge in the shadow of Your wings. (36:7)
- In the shadow of Your wings I will take refuge until destruction passes by. (57:1)
- Let me take refuge in the shelter of Your wings. (61:4)
- Because you are my help, I sing in the shadow of your wings. (63:7, NIV)
- He will cover you with His pinions, and under His wings you may seek refuge. (91:4)
- For you have made the LORD, my refuge, even the Most High, your dwelling place. (91:9)
- He who dwells in the shelter of the Most High will abide in the shadow of the Almighty. (91:1)

Jesus, from the lineage of Boaz and Ruth, will make this correlation when He pleads for Jerusalem: "Jerusalem, Jerusalem, . . . How often I wanted to gather your children together, the way a hen gathers her chicks under her wings, and you were unwilling" (Matthew 23:37).

The Kindness of Boaz

For the four or five months of barley harvest and then wheat harvest, Ruth stayed in the fields of Boaz. She remained "under his wings" where she gleaned and was protected. Boaz even provided extra for Ruth to take home to Naomi. She was offered food, water, and rest when she needed it. Boaz was generous and gave her more than she worked for. Why? Because he was strong in the Lord and was a picture of redemption.

"May I [Ruth] continue to find favor in your eyes, my lord," she said. "You have put me at ease by speaking kindly to your servant—though I do not have the standing of one of your servants."

At mealtime Boaz said to her, "Come over here. Have some bread and dip it in the wine vinegar.

"When she sat down with the harvesters, he offered her some roasted grain. She ate all she wanted and had some left over. As she got up to glean, Boaz gave orders to his men, "Let her gather among the sheaves and don't reprimand her. Even pull out some stalks for her from the bundles and leave them for her to pick up, and don't rebuke her."

So Ruth gleaned in the field until evening. Then she threshed the barley she had gathered, and it amounted to about an ephah. She carried it back to town, and her mother-in-law saw how much she had gathered. Ruth also brought out and gave her what she had left over after she had eaten enough. (Ruth 2:13–18, NIV)

Boaz served Ruth during mealtime. It was unusual to ask a gleaner to sit with the paid workers, yet he included her in the benefits of his employees. Furthermore, he commanded them not to insult her, nor rebuke her. He asked his servants to leave some of the already bundled sheaves lying on the ground for her to pick up. She was allowed to use the stones for beating the grain so that she could take the finished product home in a smaller basket, making the load easier to carry. Boaz wanted Ruth to stay close to his maid-servants so that she would be guaranteed safety. Usually gleaners went from field to field; she was allowed to remain in the fields of Boaz. She gained more grain in less time with less effort.

Just as Boaz's reputation was known and respected among his workers, so they would come to know the reputation of Ruth, the young widow who was caring for her widowed mother-in-law. Her kindness, like his, would bring further blessings.

Chapter Discussion

1.   List some qualities of Boaz from 2:4–9.

2.   In what ways was Boaz unlike other men who lived during the time of the judges?

3.   Define the characteristic of submitting to one another. Does this make sense in light of Boaz?

4.   Boaz uses the phrase "under whose wings you have come to take refuge." Describe what this means and its importance as a theme in the book of Ruth.

5.   What other references to God as El Shaddai can you find in Scripture? (You may need a concordance or Bible dictionary for this.)

6.   If you have worked outside the home, describe how you balanced your life. Remember your vocation can be both inside and outside the home.

Chapter 8

Your Choice of a Mate Matters to God

Her mother-in-law asked her, "Where did you glean today? Where did you work? Blessed be the man who took notice of you!"

Then Ruth told her mother-in-law about the one at whose place she had been working. "The name of the man I worked with today is Boaz," she said.

"The LORD bless him!" Naomi said to her daughter-in-law. "He has not stopped showing his kindness to the living and the dead." She added, "That man is our close relative; he is one of our guardian-redeemers."

Then Ruth the Moabite said, "He even said to me, 'Stay with my workers until they finish harvesting all my grain.'"

Naomi said to Ruth her daughter-in-law, "It will be good for you, my daughter, to go with the women who work for him, because in someone else's field you might be harmed."

So Ruth stayed close to the women of Boaz to glean until the barley and wheat harvests were finished. And she lived with her mother-in-law.

—Ruth 2:19–23 (NIV)

Naomi: The Matchmaker

Months into the harvest, the wheels in Naomi's mind began to turn. She was proud of Ruth and happy to have her in her life. Naomi's friends certainly saw these two women together and were amazed at their closeness. Then one day Naomi initiated a conversation that Ruth seemed not to fully pick up on.

As Ruth had toiled through the long harvest season both women realized how God had provided for them. When Naomi asked about Ruth's work in the fields and about Boaz, she was delighted to hear of his daily kindness. Naomi asked God to bless this man who had gone out of his way to care and provide for them. Then she mentioned that Boaz was a "close relative." The word she used was *goel*, which means "kinsman-redeemer."

Even though Naomi had explained the law of Levirate marriage, Ruth didn't seem to pick up on the implication of Naomi's words regarding Boaz. Ruth's heart was content. She had found friends among the friends and family of Naomi, and was happy that God had brought them to Bethlehem. She was settling into her new life among a people who called themselves "God's chosen." There is no indication that she was thinking beyond the here-and-now that she found herself in.

The Choosing of a Mate: Then and Now

Don and I dated for three months and then got married. What were we thinking!

We lived through the cultural upheaval of the fifties and sixties when rebellion against tradition was what it was all about. When I was in college in the late fifties and early sixties, women still wore girdles, hose, and skirts to class. Beginning in the sixties, women were rebelling against that dress code, so they began burning their bras. (They should have been burning their girdles.) Hair was long and unkempt, and clothes were, well . . . ugly. Students were revolting against authority, especially their parents. It was not a pretty time in American history.

I had been with Campus Crusade for Christ for four years when Don arrived on the scene. I had a career that I loved. I traveled weekly to different campuses, speaking and counseling our staff women. Both of us had had more relationships than we cared to talk about in our past. I had been engaged twice but those were very short-lived. One lasted a week and the other two months. Before meeting Don, I had sworn off boys.

Both of us had had a turnaround in our lives and wanted to live purely and solely for the Lord. Therefore, when we met and started dating, we loved our long talks together and had fun, but we did not have the "feelings" we were used to or thought we needed. But long story short, we pragmatically prayed about our relationship and knew God was in it. We committed to marry one month later. Marry we did, and the trouble began within twenty-four hours of the "I do." We didn't intend to hurt each other, but in the ensuing two years we really didn't know or understand each other, let alone what marriage was all about.

I met Don's parents one month before the wedding. Don met my parents only four days before the wedding. If our parents had been in charge of picking us for each other, we probably would not have married. But in the sixties, we weren't much into what our parents thought. Even though we were Christians and loved our thriving campus ministry, I am sure we were influenced by our surrounding culture. It was a time to *do your own thing*. When I think about how the parents of yesteryears' culture participated in choosing mates for their children, I realize we would have done well to have sought their advice and counsel.

In marriage we began to find out who we really were. Don was a huge football fan, I could not have cared less. I loved nature, he did not. I had opinions he didn't want to hear. He made decisions I didn't agree with. We were incredibly different. We didn't believe in divorce, so what were we going to do about our relationship?

Like so many couples, what we thought before marriage changed dramatically within marriage. It seems that marital problems for couples have remained fairly consistent over time, whether in an arranged marriage or in a marriage with a spouse of one's own choosing. All couples want to know how to live with an imperfect person, rarely considering that the imperfection is on both sides.

The key to successful marriage is found in the Word of God, which has not changed with the culture or the times. God's Word remains the only constant we can rely upon to fix broken people and broken marriages. For forty-five of our forty-seven years of marriage, Don and I have relied upon the unchanging, infallible, and powerful Word that constantly gives us a track to run on. Nothing else works. It doesn't matter which country you live in, what era of time, or who your spouse is, Scripture works when we follow it. We started doing marriage seminars in order to help others who were struggling. Soon we knew we had to write a discipleship course on marriage called *Two Becoming One* (8) so that others could lead and teach God's unchangeable principles.

Naomi's Era of Time

The next part of the story in the book of Ruth sounds strange to our modern ways. We choose our own spouse, so we think. We find our own jobs, so we think. We graduate from our choice of college and get certain degrees of our own choosing. We select what houses and cars to buy. We are infused with the notion that choice is our right. But is it really?

Within God's sovereignty, no matter who does the choosing, whether a parent chooses for us or we choose for ourselves, ultimately God's choice is our destiny. He has purposed a plan for each of us. He placed us in a certain part of the world, determined the era in which we would live, and set our date of birth and our date of death. Is He not also ultimately responsible then for the choice of our mate?

In previous centuries, women were generally at the mercy of their parents to choose a mate for them. Elimelech and Naomi had done this for their sons. When their sons died, making widows of Ruth and Orpah, Naomi urged them to return to their homeland and remarry. Of course we know that Orpah did go back, but Ruth stayed with Naomi. And now Naomi was once again playing the role that God had given her. She saw in Boaz the kind of man she desired for Ruth, so she became a divinely appointed matchmaker. She took this very seriously; it meant security for Ruth and for her.

Choosing a spouse for a son or daughter meant studying the character of the potential mate. Because Boaz's parents were deceased, Naomi would have had to do some extra investigating. She probably approached many in Bethlehem who knew him in order to learn of his reputation among his neighbors and relatives.

It would have been understandable if Naomi still had some reluctance even once she began to see Boaz as a potential husband for Ruth. There would have been quite an age difference between them (Boaz might well have been in his seventies). But even so, she began to see in Boaz a perfect mate for one so deserving of love and care. The age difference—which wouldn't have carried as much stigma then as now—was not nearly as important as the qualities she saw in both Ruth and Boaz, who loved and followed Yahweh.

It is also helpful to understand that this marriage would have been far less likely if Ruth had not been married before. Parents picked partners for their children, often when they were quite young. But Ruth was a widow and *available*. Furthermore, in cases of remarriage, it was perfectly acceptable for the widow to make the first move. So, what Naomi told her daughter-in-law to do next conformed to the law of levirate marriage. The woman could be the initiator in cases where a close relative is unmarried and available.

Obviously, Naomi had done research concerning the closest relatives and who would be eligible. She probably knew that there were two men who qualified, but she also knew that God had directed her and Ruth to the fields of Boaz. She could see God's guidance in this.

Did Ruth ever think of Boaz as a husband? Probably not. Did Boaz think of Ruth for a wife? Again, probably not. This was mulled over in the mind of Naomi maybe months before she approached Ruth with her idea. Ruth had not sought a man from among the young men of the fields, although it would have been acceptable for her to do so. Ruth had been modest, shy, and reserved. She had not been flirtatious or aggressive. She had only worked for the good of Naomi and herself, apparently without thought of her own future.

Naomi sensed that Ruth trusted God for the future, even if it meant no husband. She had watched how God had provided for them through gleaning. After both wheat and barley harvests, Naomi sensed it was time to act according to what she had been praying about since Ruth first "happened" to go to this wonderful man's fields.

Chapter Discussion

1. Why did Naomi pick up on God's placement, even though Ruth did not?

2. Have you ever been in a place that was out of your comfort zone, yet you knew that God was leading you to do what was right? Explain.

3. Describe how you and your husband knew you were right for each other.

4. Discuss the verses on God's Sovereignty listed in chapter six. How do those verses apply here?

Chapter 9

Your Obedience Matters to God

One day Ruth's mother-in-law Naomi said to her, "My daughter, I must find a home for you, where you will be well provided for. Now Boaz, with whose women you have worked, is a relative of ours. Tonight he will be winnowing barley on the threshing floor. Wash, put on perfume, and get dressed in your best clothes. Then go down to the threshing floor, but don't let him know you are there until he has finished eating and drinking. When he lies down, note the place where he is lying. Then go and uncover his feet and lie down. He will tell you what to do."

"I will do whatever you say," Ruth answered.

—Ruth 3:1–5 (NIV)

If brothers are living together and one of them dies without a son, his widow must not marry outside the family. Her husband's brother shall take her and marry her and fulfill the duty of a brother-in-law to her. The first son she bears shall carry on the name of the dead brother so that his name will not be blotted out from Israel.

However, if a man does not want to marry his brother's wife, she shall go to the elders at the town gate and say, "My husband's brother refuses to carry on his brother's name in Israel. He will not fulfill the duty of a brother-in-law to me." Then the elders of his town shall summon him and talk to him. If he persists in saying, "I do not want to marry her," his brother's widow shall go up to him in the presence of the elders, take off one of his sandals, spit in his face and say, "This is what is done to the man who will not build up his brother's family line." That man's line shall be known in Israel as The Family of the Unsandaled.

—Deuteronomy 25:5–10 (NIV)

Ruth had married into the family of Elimelech. Her husband Mahlon had died and left her childless. The next of kin to Elimelech and Mahlon would qualify for the marriage law described in Deuteronomy 25 because there were no children to carry on Mahlon's name and because Mahlon had no other living brother.

Naomi was past menopause, and therefore did not qualify for remarriage under this law. Ruth and Orpah both qualified, but Orpah had gone back to Moab. The question was, did Boaz qualify or was there a closer relative who would be willing to buy Elimelech's land and marry Ruth?

I am of the opinion that Ruth and Naomi didn't have as quick of a conversation as it appears in the biblical text. I believe that what we have in Scripture is a summary of lengthier conversations, perhaps many of them. Ruth and Naomi probably discussed once again the Levirate law of marriage so that both women understood and were in agreement. They would have also discussed the character of Boaz in more detail and perhaps revisited the issue of their age difference. Naomi would have taken Ruth back to some of the stories of her ancestors and the discrepancies in ages of the men and women to assure Ruth that this was perfectly acceptable. Reiteration of the law of Levirate marriage would assure Ruth that what she was about to do was also perfectly acceptable and, more importantly, honorable.

Elderly Husbands and Younger Wives

At this point it might be helpful to consider some of the husband-wife age differences within the ancestry of Naomi.

- Abraham (50) married Sarah (40)
- Isaac (40) married Rebekah (young)

- Abraham (137-170) married Keturah (second wife, child-bearing age)
- Jacob (60) married Leah and Rachel (young)
- Moses (40-70) married Zipporah (young, child-bearing age)

As you can see, it was not at all uncommon for an older man to marry a woman who was still young enough to have children. Women in their teens and twenties often married older men in order to have children that would carry on the genealogy of the paternal family. My conjecture is that Boaz may have been 70-80 and Ruth around 20 at the time of this story.

So we see Ruth being obedient once again to her aging teacher, best friend, and mother-in-law. She knew that Naomi knew best when it came to her Israelite family, neighbors, and tribal customs.

Marriage Proposal

Naomi instructed Ruth to take off her mourning clothes, bathe, put on a suitable dress, braid her hair, and wear perfume. In other words, she wanted Ruth to clean up so she didn't look like a mourner or smell like a field worker. This reminds me of the scene from the movie *Gone With the Wind* when Rhett Butler asks Scarlett to dance while she was still wearing her mourning clothes. It was scandalous. Naomi was doing a similar thing by asking Ruth to put off her mourning clothes to propose remarriage to Boaz.

In order for Ruth not to ruin her or Boaz's reputation, Naomi told her to go at dusk and wait out of sight until Boaz lies down to sleep. These were dangerous times, and marauders would often come at night to steal crops. Being an astute and watchful businessman, Boaz, along with some of his overseers, slept each night near the winnowed crops until the harvest was completed. Sleep would come quickly and easily to them because of the day's long and exhausting labor.

Once Boaz was asleep, Ruth was to lie down and uncover his feet. Naomi said, "He will tell you what to do." In other words, as a man of honor who was well versed in God's laws, Boaz would know what the next step would be, and he would inform Ruth what was to be done.

What a strange thing Naomi had asked of her, yet Ruth was ready to act. Still, I imagine that at first Ruth did some heavy-duty contemplating—and perhaps wrestling—over this strange custom. But she understood that the Levirate law was in place for protection and provision, and both she and Naomi were in need. If she did wrestle against it, she resolved matters with her great God and committed to do what she must. I don't believe she lightly submitted without fully understanding the law and understanding why Naomi was asking this of her. She was brave but she knew the consequences if Boaz reprimanded her. However, she ultimately responded: "I will do whatever you say."

Imagine the scene: Ruth's heart beats wildly, she bathes, changes clothes, and with trepidation goes to the threshing floor to await darkness, hoping no one would see her.

So she went down to the threshing floor and did everything her mother-in-law told her to do.

When Boaz had finished eating and drinking and was in good spirits, he went over to lie down at the far end of the grain pile. Ruth approached quietly, uncovered his feet and lay down. In the middle of the night something startled the man; he turned—and there was a woman lying at his feet!

"Who are you?" he asked.

"I am your servant Ruth," she said. "Spread the corner of your garment over me, since you are a guardian-redeemer of our family."

"The LORD bless you, my daughter," he replied. "This kindness is greater than that which you showed earlier: You have not run after the younger men, whether rich or poor. And now, my daughter, don't be afraid. I will do for you all you ask. All the people of my town know that you are a woman of noble character. Although it is true that I am a guardian-redeemer of our family, there is another who is more closely related than I. Stay here for the night, and in the morning if he wants to do his duty as your guardian-redeemer, good; let him redeem you. But if he is not willing, as surely as the LORD lives I will do it. Lie here until morning."

So she lay at his feet until morning, but got up before anyone could be recognized; and he said, "No one must know that a woman came to the threshing floor." (Ruth 3:6–14, NIV)

Ruth explicitly did all that Naomi had instructed. When Boaz awoke during the night—perhaps because his feet were cold from his blanket being removed—he quickly realized that a woman was lying at his feet. When Ruth told him she was his servant and then made the bold statement, "Spread the corner of your garment over me, since you are a kinsman-redeemer of our family," Boaz was well aware of her intent for him to become her permanent protector and provider.

Ruth's actions invoked the same picture of El Shaddai that Boaz had previously blessed her with, that of coming under the wings of God. It is also a beautiful depiction of marriage. The husband is the Christ-figure (the protector), and the wife is the protected one (the church). Together they form a oneness that both pictures marriage and foreshadows the unity of Christ and the church throughout eternity. This is why Paul wrote in Ephesians 5:32, "This mystery [the oneness of a man and woman in marriage] is great; but I am speaking with reference to Christ and the church."

When Ruth asked Boaz to be her husband/guardian-redeemer, Boaz replied, "There is another man who is a closer relative than I." He explained that he would first need to see if that male relative would fulfill the role of guardian-redeemer. Boaz was well aware of the law of Levirate marriage, so he informed Ruth of this fact in order to protect her reputation, lest anyone misunderstand or accuse her of wrongdoing.

Don and I liken Ruth and Boaz to the modern-day story of some close friends. Arlen had been married before and had children. His first wife died of heart disease when they were in their late 50s. Carol was a young single lady who helped in our ministry and with our four children. Both of these people were godly, walking with the Lord and following Him. Carol had lived with us in Virginia for several years, and had spent time with Marian, Arlen's wife. After a time, Carol moved back to Little Rock, where we first met. Six months after Marian's death, Arlen came to our house for dinner and in the conversation asked how old Carol was. She was considerably younger, in her 30s. We saw his wheels turning and told him to pray about it and let the Lord work. Unbeknownst to him, Carol had begun to have fleeting thoughts of Arlen and wondered what *that* was all about. When we flew into Little Rock for a conference sometime later, Carol picked us up and proceeded to ask us how old Arlen was. When that happened, we knew God was working on both sides of the aisle.

We then strategized in secret phone calls with Arlen and Carol (no other friends knew) how to get them together so they could talk. We planned a vacation and took Arlen and Carol along with our family of six. As we watched, God spoke loud and clear to both of them. Our whole family participated in their wedding six months later. They have now been married for over thirty years. She is the second mother to his three grown children and the grandmother of their grandchildren.

Why do I tell this story? Because God still works the same way with every couple He brings together. He works on *both* individuals to confirm His will. Both the man and the woman must be in agreement with God's leading and His choice of their mate. It was no different for Arlen and Carol than it was for Boaz and Ruth.

Commitment vs. Feelings

In Israel, a guardian-redeemer was a very important person. His role had nothing to do with what we would think of as "love" for the bride-to-be, although God would bring that in time. This had everything to do with the genealogy God was working out through each tribe and family in Israel. As we know, Ruth was willing to put her own future on the line for the sake of Elimelech, her deceased father-in-law, and Mahlon, her deceased husband. That Boaz was an honorable and godly man was a blessing that was not always the case in this type of marriage. He expressed his willingness, but under the law the other "closer relative" would have to back out of the arrangement before Boaz could step in to fulfill the duty of guardian-redeemer.

Again, we are not talking about *feelings* of love, but about an obligation. In our Western culture, we expect feelings to come first, and then a commitment. Historically, and still in certain parts of the world, love *followed* the commitment. The covenant of marriage undergirded feelings and changing circumstances.

Notice that Boaz's reply was a blessing: "The LORD bless you, my daughter" and a recognition of Ruth's character: "This kindness is greater than that which you showed earlier [to Naomi]." Ruth had done the honorable thing "by not going after younger men, either rich or poor." Boaz complimented her noble ways and would protect her reputation until the matter could be discussed openly at the gates of the city (the equivalent of a court of law). There the guardian-redeemer would be publically and legally appointed according to Levirate law. Boaz then gave Ruth some grain that she had not gleaned. This small act of generosity was an indication to both Ruth and Naomi that they could depend on him to personally resolve the matter as quickly as possible.

Don't you believe that Ruth and Naomi earnestly hoped and prayed that it would be Boaz who would be their kinsman-redeemer? I doubt that they got much sleep that night. Perhaps Boaz didn't either.

Elders' Meeting

Now Boaz went up to the gate and sat down there, and behold, the close relative of whom Boaz spoke was passing by, so he said, "Turn aside, friend, sit down here." And he turned aside and sat down. He took ten men of the elders of the city and said, "Sit down here." So they sat down. Then he said to the closest relative, "Naomi, who has come back from the land of Moab, has to sell the piece of land which belonged to our brother Elimelech. "So I thought to inform you, saying, 'Buy it before those who are sitting here, and before the elders of my people. If you will redeem it, redeem it; but if not, tell me that I may know; for there is no one but you to redeem it, and I am after you.'" And he said, "I will redeem it." Then Boaz said, "On the day you buy the field from the hand of Naomi, you must also acquire Ruth the Moabitess, the widow of the deceased, in order to raise up the name of the deceased on his inheritance." The closest relative said, "I cannot redeem it for myself, because I would jeopardize my own inheritance. Redeem it for yourself; you may have my right of redemption, for I cannot redeem it."

Now this was the custom in former times in Israel concerning the redemption and the exchange of land to confirm any matter: a man removed his sandal and gave it to another; and this was the manner of attestation in Israel. So the closest relative said to Boaz, "Buy it for yourself." And he removed his sandal. (Ruth 4:1–8)

Boaz did the proper thing by asking the closer relative to buy Elimelech's property. But when this man agreed to buy it, he didn't realize that he would also have to marry the heir's widow Ruth, and also assume care for Elimelech's widow, Naomi. Out of concern that a levirate marriage could limit the size of his estate, he declined to become the kinsman-redeemer. (The exact reason for his refusal is unclear. One possible scenario is that this man already had children. If he already had a son, and if he and Ruth were to have a son, Ruth's son would inherit all of Elimelech's property as well as a portion of the man's property, thereby reducing the inheritance of his other children.) For whatever reason, he stepped aside, yielding the role of redeemer to Boaz. I gather from this that Boaz did not have living children; nowhere in Scripture are other children mentioned.

Contract with Sandals

Sandals were personal property. Because of the daily wear, sandals would take on the unique shape of the owner's feet, and his footprint would form an indelible impression inside the sandal. (Could this have been that era's version of finger-printing? Possibly.) A sandal was used as evidence that property had indeed been transferred from one person to another. The seller of the property would give one sandal and keep the other, making it possible to identify him by comparing the sandals with each other. The sandal was proof that a legal transaction had occurred.

Land transactions were always public, with witnesses, so that if a dispute arose later, the witnesses could be called. When Boaz accepted the sandal from the closer relative, he was stating publically his intent to redeem the land belonging to Elimelech, to care for Naomi, and to marry Ruth. Boaz followed the laws of Israel concerning property and contracts. In our courts of law today we follow a similar pattern, including contracts and witnesses.

Blessing from the Elders to Boaz and Ruth

Then Boaz said to the elders and all the people, "You are witnesses today that I have bought from the hand of Naomi all that belonged to Elimelech and all that belonged to Chilion and Mahlon. "Moreover, I have acquired Ruth the Moabitess, the widow of Mahlon, to be my wife in order to raise up the name of the deceased on his inheritance, so that the name of the deceased will not be cut off from his brothers or from the court of his birth place; you are witnesses today." All the people who were in the court, and the elders, said, "We are witnesses. May the LORD make the woman who is coming into your home like Rachel and Leah, both of whom built the house of Israel; and may you achieve wealth in Ephrathah and become famous in Bethlehem. Moreover, may your house be like the house of Perez whom Tamar bore to Judah, through the offspring which the LORD will give you by this young woman." (Ruth 4:9–12)

The elders and other witnesses voiced their consent with a blessing to Boaz and his household, calling special attention to the genealogy of the tribe of Judah. Elimelech, Mahlon, and Boaz were all from this tribe, as were the elders who spoke.

Boaz did indeed become famous in Bethlehem. This story has been told for centuries as a testament to the Lord's faithfulness to His people. In the midst of a perverse generation, God's light shined upon a godly family heritage. It's interesting that the blessing included the child or children that would come from this union. Ruth was likely thought to be barren since she and Mahlon had conceived no children. Would God open her womb? Would there be more to the story of Boaz and Ruth? What would come of their union?

Rachael and Leah

Rachael and Leah were sisters who married the same man, Jacob. Along with their two maids, these four women bore Jacob twelve sons and a daughter. Jacob's name was later changed to Israel. His sons became the fathers of the twelve tribes of Israel. These twelve tribes comprise the whole of the Jewish settlement in Canaan under the leadership of Joshua. The town of Bethlehem was settled by the tribe of Judah, son of Jacob. In blessing Boaz and Ruth, the elders were calling upon God to produce a lineage from them that would go down in history. Their blessings were prophetical as centuries later would prove in the coming of the Messiah.

Tamar

It's interesting that Tamar is mentioned in this blessing. Tamar was a Canaanite woman who married Judah's son, Er. For whatever reason, Er didn't want children and would not consummate their union. God intervened and took his life. Tamar was then given to the next son who did the same thing. God was again displeased and killed him as well. When Judah didn't step in to correct this wrongdoing in his family, Tamar disguised herself and played the prostitute with Judah. She conceived and bore him a son named Perez, and it was through him that the family line continued. Judah confessed that Tamar was more righteous than he because she followed the law of Levirate marriage, even when he was unwilling. The importance of following family laws was paramount, and the honorable thing was to marry within the original family structure.

Kinsman-Redeemer and the Messiah

As with all books in the Old Testament, Ruth foreshadows Jesus the Messiah and our redemption through Him. This foreshadowing is beautifully done in the book of Ruth through Boaz, the kinsman-redeemer. Consider what must be true in order for one to qualify as a kinsman-redeemer (*goel*). See how each of these "qualifications" was met by Boaz, and also by Christ.

1. He must be related by blood. (Deuteronomy 25:5, 7–10; John 1:14; Romans 1:3; Philippians 2:5–8; Hebrews 2:14–15)
2. He must be able to pay the price of redemption. (Ruth 2:1; 1 Peter 1:18–19)
3. He must be free to redeem. (Christ was free from sin—2 Corinthians 5:21)
4. He must be willing to redeem. (Ruth 3:11; Matthew 20:28; John 10:15, 18; Hebrews 10:7) (9)

God sent His only Son to earth to redeem us from sin and from spending eternity in hell without Him. As the Son of God, Jesus is the closest kinsman to God. In becoming a man, Jesus became our closest kinsman as well. The kinsman-redeemer is a perfect picture of Christ the Messiah, dying on a cross, shedding His blood to redeem us. Ruth was bought with a price. We are bought with a price. Boaz paid for Ruth from his own wealth. Jesus paid for our sins with his own blood. Boaz gave so that he could win her. Jesus gave so that He could win us.

The book of Ruth presents a picture of the divine plan to rescue us from a life of barrenness, pity, scorn, loneliness, and emptiness and bring us into a life of fullness, joy, and blessing.

Remember that you were at that time separate from Christ, excluded from the commonwealth of Israel, and strangers to the covenants of promise, having no hope and without God in the world. But now in Christ Jesus you who formerly were far off have been brought near by the blood of Christ. (Ephesians 2:12–13)

We have before us a picture of Christ and the church. Boaz did everything to win the hand of Ruth. Christ did everything to woo and win us from darkness to light. Boaz followed the law. Christ fulfilled the law. Boaz demonstrated the nature of Christ; he was noble, righteous, gracious, tactful, caring, giving, generous, and protective.

If Boaz is a picture of Christ, Ruth is a picture of you and me (the church, the bride). She was rescued from a pagan culture, married into the family of God, and gleaned in the fields of her beloved even before she came fully under his wing. She fell at his feet, and he embraced her with his arms outstretched in covenant marriage.

El Shaddai, with his wings outstretched has wooed and won his bride. We have fallen at the feet of our great Redeemer, Jesus Christ. Remember that we were in a barren place, in a land where we didn't belong. We were brought home to a place of belonging and to a God who loves deeply. We have finally relaxed in the arms of our great Lover. And in that place we bear fruit.

Chapter Discussion

1. What is the significance of Ruth using the "wings" terminology with Boaz?

2. In what ways did Ruth's proposal reveal what kind of man she believed Boaz to be?

3. What is the importance of commitment vs. feelings when it comes to love and marriage?

4. What does the book of Ruth reveal about our redemption through Christ? What does it teach concerning the Messiah?

Chapter 10

Your Legacy Matters to God

So Boaz took Ruth, and she became his wife.
—Ruth 4:13

The Wedding

What a joyful pair. Can you imagine the scene? Boaz, the wealthy landowner, takes the beautiful young woman into his arms, and dances with her. She reaches up and wipes a tear away and lovingly kisses his weathered cheeks. The townspeople look on, happy that they have been a part of this wonderful love story. Naomi's friends, who helped plan and prepare the wedding, whisper softly as they watch in amazement. Boaz's workers and their families are also in attendance, along with all of Bethlehem, it seems. Nobody wanted to miss this wedding of all weddings.

Naomi looks on and smiles, her heart filled with wonder at the sight of her dear Ruth in the strong arms of Boaz. She remembers all the years and the tears in Moab, and wishes that her Elimelech were here to share in this wonderful day. Can this really be happening? Her eyes moisten as she looks up to heaven and offers quiet gratitude to El Shaddai.

Marriage was designed by God before sin entered the world (Genesis 1–2), and it brings beautiful completion to both the man and the woman. Boaz and Ruth depict the plan of God to reflect His image through their marriage. This is why we so love the way this story ends. Boaz represents the strong character of Christ, and Ruth represents the church that responds to His love and comes to life because of it. Together, as husband and wife, they would glorify the Lord, knowing that He had orchestrated the events that brought them together. God's purposes through their marriage would have kingdom connotations for future generations. As He had designed their past, so He would their future.

Naomi Gains a Son

> So Boaz took Ruth, and she became his wife, and he went in to her. And the LORD enabled her to conceive, and she gave birth to a son. Then the women said to Naomi, "Blessed is the LORD who has not left you without a redeemer today, and may his name become famous in Israel. May he also be to you a restorer of life and a sustainer of your old age; for your daughter-in-law, who loves you and is better to you than seven sons, has given birth to him." (Ruth 4:13–15)

Ruth gave Naomi more joy, more companionship, more care, and more love than she could ever have imagined. Naomi's friends cannot compliment Ruth enough. I think of how God gave Job and Mrs. Job another seven sons and three daughters after their terrible losses. Ruth was more joy to Naomi than if God had given her seven (perfect number) sons!

> Then Naomi took the child and laid him in her lap, and became his nurse. The neighbor women gave him a name, saying, "A son has been born to Naomi!" So they named him Obed. He is the father of Jesse, the father of David. (4:16–17)

When God allowed Ruth to conceive, Naomi must have been beside herself. She was going to become a grandmother! God was at work, both in opening Ruth's barren womb and in bringing along this child who would continue the lineage that would lead to the birth of Christ. The child had to come from Boaz (of the tribe of Judah) and Ruth.

This is the only time in the Bible that a name is given to a child not by his parents or God, but by neighbor women. And what a name they gave him: Obed, which means "servant." He is the summation of all that had happened in this small family, and I believe is a foretaste of what was to come a couple of centuries later in this same little town of Bethlehem. A true Servant would come in the form of a baby boy and show us just what servanthood really means.

Obed: A Fitting Name

Obed (servant) sums up the entire book of Ruth.

> Naomi served Ruth in winning her to the Lord and discipling her.
> Ruth served Naomi by going to Bethlehem and gleaning for their survival.
> Boaz served Ruth in giving her grain in abundance.
> Ruth served Boaz in giving him honor in the marriage proposal.
> Boaz served Ruth in taking her under his wing for provision and protection.
> Naomi served Ruth and Boaz by becoming more than a grandmother to their son. She became his nurse, mentor, and friend.
> Obed probably served Naomi in her old age with joy.
> Obed probably served Boaz in his old age with joy.
> Obed probably served Ruth for the rest of her life in caring for her.

The great suffering Servant of Isaiah 53, a descendant of Boaz, will be our King of kings and Lord of lords. But first, He was Servant. Joy in life comes from giving and serving others. No matter what we have, no matter what we are going through, God gets us out of ourselves when we think of and give to others. Our greatest Servant taught us how to serve and love with joy: "It is more blessed to give than to receive" (Acts 20:35).

Camaraderie of Women

No wonder it was the friends of Naomi that gave Obed his name. They even said, "Naomi has a son!" Isn't it strange that the neighbor women would be more excited for Naomi than for Ruth? This book begins and ends with Naomi. But Ruth doesn't seem to mind the attention Naomi receives. She takes it in stride and is proud to watch Naomi love on her baby boy.

As Naomi tenderly takes this young child into her arms she also takes him into her heart. Many years earlier she had given birth to two sons of her own. Her dreams had been shattered by their deaths, and her heart still had a hole. She often thought of dear Elimelech and how she would love to have been able to share the joy of a grandchild with him. The hole in her heart was mending even though there would always be longing for the past. It will be filled with new wonder and new joy as she bonds with little Obed.

Naomi could dream again. Obed filled a vacuum. What joy welled up in her when she held him and kissed his sweet cheeks. She would one day teach him the same stories she told to her sons and daughters-in-law. She would teach and she would mentor and she would love. God is good. Naomi was sheltered under His wings so that she might shelter another under her wings.

I love what this story says about being a grandmother. I love the blessing the women gave to Naomi because of this precious, long-awaited baby boy: "May he be to you a restorer of life and a sustainer of your old age."

What a powerful statement for grandparents. Grandchildren do just that, they make us feel young. We do things with them that we thought we were past doing. We play, laugh, and tumble (if we can get down and back up again). We have someone to live for. They keep us thinking young. They restore a part of our lives and they sustain us as we age. How blessed we are to be grandparents.

I loved my own children, but got uptight way too often. I adore my grand-children . . . and can give them back to their parents so I don't tend to get as stressed. I enjoy them. The statement has a grain of truth: "Grandchildren are so much fun I wish we had had them first." I believe that our job is not finished when our children are grown. We must help raise the next generation of disciples who will become kingdom builders. Micah 6:8 says, "And what does the LORD require of you but to do justice, to love kindness, and to walk humbly with your God?" As grandparents we are to help nurture, teach, and encourage the next generation to know the Lord and to learn to walk in His ways.

Psalm 78:2–8 also gives instruction to grandparents.

> I will open my mouth in a parable;
> I will utter dark sayings of old,
> Which we have heard and known,
> And our fathers have told us.
> We will not conceal them from their children,
> But tell to the generation to come the praises of the LORD,
> And His strength and His wondrous works that He has done.
>
> For He established a testimony in Jacob
> And appointed a law in Israel,
> Which He commanded our fathers
> That they should teach them to their children,
> That the generation to come might know, even the children yet to be born,
> That they may arise and tell them to their children,
> That they should put their confidence in God
> And not forget the works of God,
> But keep His commandments,
> And not be like their fathers,
> A stubborn and rebellious generation,
> A generation that did not prepare its heart
> And whose spirit was not faithful to God.

This passage talks about four generations of teaching, and Naomi is a clear example. She knew that with the raising of her sons she was not finished. With the birth of Obed she still had work to do. And it was a wise mother, Ruth, who wanted and allowed Naomi's involvement. Grandparents are incredibly important. So often they want to "check out" and not be involved. I have personally been convicted that my grandchildren need input from Don and me. Our grown children still need our input, example, and encouragement while raising their children. It's a wise grandparent who sees her value to the generations who come after. Far too many grandparents shirk this responsibility and are not very involved.

Most of my eleven grandchildren have sat with me and asked me wonderful questions about the Lord. What a privilege to talk one on one to each of them. I know my grown children love watching the relationship we have with each young child. I want to create memories that they will hold dear. I also know there is coming a day when their peers will be more important to them than spending time with grandparents, so I want to make the most of my time with them while they are young. God has honored the time we've spent together, and my heart is full each time it happens. Don has such wisdom to offer the children, especially as they enter the teen years. He has had some very special time with the older grandkids, helping give direction for the coming turbulent teen years.

Don and I also believe that marriage is so important that we have volunteered to stay with the children of each of the four families so the couples can have alone time, rest time, and refreshment for their marriages. Grandparents who are physically able would do well to help strengthen the marriages of their grown children. Healthy marriages promote healthy kids. It may not always be possible because of health issues or geographical distances, but let them know you want to do this, even if you can't.

Importance of Genealogy

Today, we seem to be enthralled with finding out about people in our past. Ancestry research is big business. Why? Because the past connects us to the future and to our own value as human beings. Knowing the stories of those who came before us gives meaning to our own.

I love the story of my great-great-great-grandfather, Peter Penner, who seemingly died at age fourteen when he was bucked off his horse and hit his head. He was laid out on a table for people to come by and pay their last respects. On the third day, just before they were to bury him, he opened his eyes. Because he lived, I am here today. So I thank God for those relatives and friends who didn't bury him alive! Literally thousands of his posterity owe their lives to God, who woke Peter Penner up just in time.

Genealogy is important in Scripture. Whole books are devoted just to it (for example, 1 and 2 Chronicles). So often in teaching and reading Scripture, we have the tendency to skip past all the names and get to the meat of the passage. Has it occurred to you why genealogies are included?

The genealogical records were kept from Genesis to Nehemiah, and put in scrolls in the Tabernacle and then the Temple. Tribes had to verify who they came from. When Jesus Christ appeared, He had to prove that He was from Abraham, Isaac, and Jacob, and then narrow that further to the tribe of Judah, and to King David. His lineage was so important that both Gospel writers Matthew (Joseph's lineage) and Luke (Mary's lineage) devoted space to recording it. Prophecy foretold which family tribe the Messiah would come from, and which king would be part of his DNA.

Interestingly, the book of Ruth provides us with a record of King David's family tree. Remember at the beginning of this book Biblical history was likened to a puzzle? The top of the box is the genealogy of the Messiah. The book of Ruth now puts this piece into the puzzle to show where it belongs.

> Now these are the generations of Perez: to Perez was born Hezron, and to Hezron was born Ram, and to Ram, Amminadab, and to Amminadab was born Nahshon, and to Nahshon, Salmon, and to Salmon was born Boaz, and to Boaz, Obed, and to Obed was born Jesse, and to Jesse, David. (Ruth 4:18–22)

Conclusion

From start to finish in this short book, we see the story of our own conversion. It parallels the teaching of Ephesians 2:12: "Remember that you were at that time separate from Christ, excluded from the commonwealth of Israel, and strangers to the covenants of promise, having no hope and without God in the world."

One March day in 2003, as I was flying I recorded my thoughts on a paper. "Lord, this is an incredibly beautiful planet from this vantage point. I see the orange-red sunset on the horizon. It's peaceful and serene, very calm somehow. But I know that below every single person is in the process of a crisis of one sort or another – with a husband, a child, an ailing parent, a business deal gone bad, a presentation to sell a product, a child on drugs, a marriage gone sour, a check book with very little in it, an insurance company who won't pay a bill, a war in Iraq. Yet I see the lights below. It's a work of art in design–a pattern. Your view of my life must be like my view of earth right now. Its design, its beauty, it's peace–it will all work together for good. You see the complete picture, I see the details. You are in control–I don't have control. I only see the cover. You have the title page and all the chapters of my life written out (C. S. Lewis). You are the Great Author. You are writing My story. I've only read 62 years of it. But I know I have a story that will go on for eternity. (How boring! Guess You don't think so.) So here's the rest of my life, Lord, write upon the pages as You see fit–it's Yours!"

Like Ruth, we were aliens to God, miserable, without hope, in famine and distress with no kinsman-redeemer in sight. Then we were rescued from a life of shame to the great life with God in Christ. We fall at the feet of Christ, our Redeemer, and ask Him to put His covering over us. He is kind. He takes us into His heart. He provides for us and protects us. He ultimately takes us to His Father's house where we will live with Him forever. He is the Groom. We are His bride. There is something very beautiful about always being the bride, always being in the state of beauty we were meant to be. Under His wings we will remain because He is forever our El Shaddai.

I like what Nicole Nordman wrote in her poem, *When Love Sees You.* (10)

. . . .

Tell me your story,
Show me your wounds,
And I'll show you what Love sees
When Love looks at you.
Hand me the pieces, broken and bruised,
And I'll show you what Love sees
When Love sees you.

. . . .

I see what I made in your mother's womb.

I see the day I fell in love with you.

I see your tomorrows, nothing left to chance;

I see my Father's fingerprints.

I see your story, I see My name

Written on every beautiful page.

You see the struggle, you see the shame,

I see the reason I came.

I came for your story . . . .

The Story *Is* in the Names

So the meaning of this incredible story is indeed in the names. The Lord Jesus fulfills every name written in these four chapters of Ruth. As His image bearers, He wants us also to fulfill the meaning of these names in our own lives.

As God continues to write *your* story,

May you say with *Elimelech* that "My God is King."

May you be beautiful and pleasant like *Naomi*.

May you be a friend of God and a friend of sinners, like *Ruth*.

May you be strong in the Lord like *Boaz*.

And may you, like *Obed*, serve your God faithfully all the days of your life.

May you stay under the wings of the Almighty through both joy and sorrow.

For *El Shaddai* is worthy of your praise and worthy of your worship.

Chapter Discussion

1. What makes Naomi a central character in the book of Ruth?

2. What promises do grandchildren bring to us in our old age?

3. Why is grandparenting such an important job?

4. Define the meaning of each of the following names:

    Elimelech
    Naomi
    Ruth
    Boaz
    Obed

5. Read Ephesians 2:12. Describe how this verse parallels the story of the book of Ruth.

6. In your opinion, what is the overarching theme of this book? (There may be more than one.)

Appendix

Your Spoken Words Matter to God: The Power of Blessing

We cried the most with our last. It wasn't because she was the last one of our four to go off to college. It wasn't because Don and I were afraid of an empty nest. It was because we did something with her that we hadn't known to do with the other three. We discovered the power of blessing.

I had been studying and teaching on Ruth for many years. I kept seeing oral blessings flowing out of the mouth of it's characters but somehow missed the purpose and meaning. Why would the author of this book give us so many examples of blessing? What was so important and life-giving about blessing?

Then something happened in my own life that brought about an "ah-ha" moment. About twenty years ago, I heard a message on television that both stunned and fascinated me. Reverend Bill Ligon (11) of Valdosta, Georgia, simply talked about "how" to bless your children. Until then, no one had ever taught me about the purpose or the power of incorporating spoken blessings into our family structure. I am a visual learner so hearing and watching the "how to's" was incredibly important.

A few weeks later, as we were driving our youngest daughter, Tiffany, to Auburn University for her freshman year, we listened to Rev. Ligon's message together. When it finished, I asked Tiffany if she would like us to bless her as she went off to college. She said, "I was hoping you would do this for me."

Don was driving and with eyes on the road, laid his right hand on Tiffany's shoulder as I placed my hands on both her shoulders. We blessed

Tiffany: (1) for who she was to us, (2) for how she had graced our home for eighteen years, and (3) for what we wanted to see God do in her life in the next four years. When we were finished, all three of us were crying. It was a very moving experience.

When we got home, Don and I began a study of blessing in the Bible. We have since used "the blessing" to bring lots of joy and hope to our family and to others.

In my study and speaking on the book of Ruth, I began to see clearly that people in the tribe of Judah practiced a way of life using the principles of speaking blessings to one another. Because we had begun our study of the Scriptures concerning blessing, these phrases simply began to stand out to me.

Blessings in the Book of Ruth

The book of Ruth is one of the most comprehensive books in the Bible on the subject of blessing. Within four short chapters there are some fourteen blessings given by different people for different purposes.

Chapter One

1:5 – May the LORD deal kindly with you

1:6 – May the LORD grant that you may find rest

1:17 – May the LORD do to me

Chapter Two

2:4 – May the LORD be with you; May the Lord bless you

2:12 – May the LORD reward your work; May your wages be full from the LORD

2:19 – May he be blessed who took notice

2:20 – May he be blessed for his kindness

Chapter Three

3:10 – May you be blessed of the LORD for your kindness

Chapter Four

    4:11 – May the Lord make the woman like Rachael and Leah;
        May you achieve wealth

    4:12 – May your house be like the house of Perez

    4:14 – May his name become famous in Israel

    4:15 – May he be to you a restorer of life and a sustainer of your
        old age

Who blessed whom in the book of Ruth?

    Mother-in-law to daughters-in-law

    Boaz (employer) to employees

    Employees to Boaz

    Boaz to Ruth

    Naomi about Boaz

    Elders to Boaz

    Townspeople to Boaz and Ruth

    Women friends of Naomi blessing Obed

Learning to Bless

1. What does it mean to bless?

To *bless* means to place a high value upon, to compliment, to encourage, or to speak hopefully of a person's future. In order to understand blessing, we should consider the opposite, which is to insult.

    To *insult* is to speak or act in a way that hurts and causes damage to another person. If you give an insult, either in words or actions, you may in turn get an insult back, creating an insult cycle. In this case, you would be wise to heed the words of 1 Peter 3:8–12:

    To sum up, all of you be harmonious, sympathetic, brotherly, kind-
    hearted, and humble in spirit; not returning evil for evil or insult for

insult, but giving a blessing instead; for you were called for the very purpose that you might inherit a blessing. For,

"THE ONE WHO DESIRES LIFE, TO LOVE AND SEE GOOD DAYS,
MUST KEEP HIS TONGUE FROM EVIL AND HIS LIPS FROM SPEAKING DECEIT.
"HE MUST TURN AWAY FROM EVIL AND DO GOOD;
HE MUST SEEK PEACE AND PURSUE IT.
"FOR THE EYES OF THE LORD ARE TOWARD THE RIGHTEOUS,
AND HIS EARS ATTEND TO THEIR PRAYER,
BUT THE FACE OF THE LORD IS AGAINST THOSE WHO DO EVIL."

2. Blessing vs. Insulting

Blessings bring forward momentum in families and lives are positively changed. A blessing carries with it compliments, encouragement, and value, which affect a person's life for years. Positive words spoken to a spouse, a child, or a friend encourage growth and maturity. God promises that we will love life, age well, and have less stress. God hears our prayers and answers them. He waits for us to bless others and He responds by blessing us.

On the other hand, insults hurt others and ourselves. I believe they hurt God as well, and He is not free to work in our lives. Insults can have lasting effects on relationships; being insulting in one relationship can impact other relationships.

We can be a negative or a positive influence in a person's life, and both influences have a tendency to keep going. Take, for example, Ephesians 6:4, "Fathers do not provoke your children to anger." When fathers bark orders at their children, don't speak kindly to them, put them down, or never tell them they are loved and appreciated, it causes anger in the child. Eventually, what relationship there might have been becomes deeply scarred, making it extremely difficult to heal no matter how hard the father tries. The better way is for fathers to talk and listen and value their child. When that child is older, he or she is far more likely to talk to, listen to, and value the parent. We have a lasting impact on a child's life by how we treat them when they are young. Do you bless, or do you insult?

3. How do we bless?

Patterns for blessing are found in both the Old and New Testaments. God was the first to bless His children in Genesis 1: "And God blessed them; and God said to them, "Be fruitful and multiply and fill the earth." God's intention was that we would reproduce godly children who would also reflect the relationship between the Father, Son, and Holy Spirit. Children were intended to be blessings in our lives.

Patterned after God's example, we are to bless our own children. Throughout the book of Genesis fathers gave blessings to their sons regarding their futures.

- First, God blessed Abraham telling him he would be the father of a people too numerous to number, and that he would be a blessing to future generations.
- Abraham blessed Isaac, passing down God's blessing to him.
- Isaac blessed both of his sons, Jacob and Esau, telling them they would become fathers of multitudes.
- God blessed Jacob when changing his name to Israel.
- Jacob, when dying, blessed his twelve sons, foretelling their futures by their already demonstrated character.
- Jacob blessed his grandsons, Manasseh and Ephraim, Joseph's sons.

In Numbers 6:23–27 God tells Moses, "Speak to Aaron and to his sons, saying, 'Thus you shall bless the sons of Israel. You shall say to them: The LORD bless you and keep you; the LORD make His face shine upon you, and be gracious to you; the LORD lift up His countenance upon you, and give you peace.' So shall they invoke My name on the sons of Israel, and then I will bless them."

Jesus blessed the children in Mark 10:16: "And He took them in his arms and began blessing them, laying His hands on them." Here we have the physical act of laying hands upon the person while giving a blessing. We are not told what Jesus said.

When Jesus was leaving His disciples and returning to heaven, the Scripture says, "And He lifted up His hands and blessed them. While He was blessing them, He parted from them . . . And they, after worshiping Him, returned to Jerusalem with great joy and were continually in the temple, praising God" (Luke 24:50–53).

4. What is involved in giving a blessing?

Parents are usually the ones to start a tradition of blessing their children and grandchildren. This can start as early as the birth of a child, and continue with blessing ceremonies throughout the child's life. Here is what a blessing may look like.

A. Choose one person and seat them in the middle of the group.
B. Gently place your hands on their head or shoulders; touch is important.

1.   Each person speaks words of appreciation, expressing high value. (For example: call attention to their positive qualities or express how they have been a blessing in the past.)

2.   Ask God to bless them in the future. Most Old Testament phrases begin with "May the Lord bless you with/by . . ." This is an act of asking God's favor and gifts to be placed upon them, specifically and generally. Create a positive vision for their future, with concrete hopes for them. Pray they will have a sense of being chosen by God.

5. When to Bless

A. Christmas Celebration

We have four children. At the time of this blessing ceremony all four were either in college or had just completed college. None were married. Don and I wrote out blessings for each one. We praised each one for who they were and how they had blessed our lives and family. We then asked God to bless their futures, including jobs, mates, and children. This was a very moving experience for our whole family. Tears of joy were shed. Each one appreciated our words of affirmation over their lives, as well as what was spoken to them from their siblings.

B. Wedding Rehearsal Dinner

This was also a very moving time for our family. After their friends had made their comments, we had parents from the bride and groom stand behind the couple as they sat at the head table. Laying our hands on their shoulders, all four parents spoke blessings on them, and gave them written copies to keep.

An example:

Todd and Sara, may you always find adoration in each other. May the two of you be an example of reflecting the image of God. May you have fun together in marriage, in life, and someday in old age. May each chapter of your lives become memories to share with your children. May you reproduce children who come to know Christ in a personal way at an early age. May you set the example of a Christ-like walk so your children can follow you. May you teach each child to honor God by his words and behavior. May you cherish each child for their uniqueness, knowing God has made each one special. May your grandchildren love coming to your home to be taught by you, to have fun with you, and to be mentored by you. May you have joy in your careers as you honor God by your words and actions. May you rule carefully over that which God entrusts to you.

C. Special Occasions

Blessing can also be extended to relatives and friends. Occasions when we have done this include leaving home for college, starting a new job or career, writing a letter or card to a bride and groom, birth of a child or grandchild, dedication ceremonies, baptism of older children, and the completion of a marriage class.

Be creative, knowing that God takes very seriously the blessings we give. He honors what steps we take to bless others. We serve a great God who desires to bless us so that we can become a blessing to others.

We were delighted that at the end of her four years at Auburn University, every blessing we gave to Tiffany actually occurred. Many of the blessings we gave to our children that Christmas when they were all single, actually happened. All four children married spouses who love and honor the Lord above all else. Every marriage is a happy one, not without trials or problems, but happy. We praise God that He honored our steps of faith and blessed our children.

Conclusion

May you be blessed as you embark upon your own blessing ceremonies for your family and friends. May God be honored in your lives as you honor one another. Remember, as we bless, we receive blessings in return. And the cycle continues.

Read Deuteronomy 28:1–12 below. This was given to Israel, but as believers we can claim the blessings written here as well.

"Now it shall be, if you diligently obey the LORD your God, being careful to do all His commandments which I command you today, the LORD your God will set you high above all the nations of the earth. All these blessings will come upon you and overtake you if you obey the LORD your God:

"Blessed shall you be in the city, and blessed shall you be in the country.

"Blessed shall be the offspring of your body and the produce of your ground and the offspring of your beasts, the increase of your herd and the young of your flock.

"Blessed shall be your basket and your kneading bowl.

"Blessed shall you be when you come in, and blessed shall you be when you go out.

"The LORD shall cause your enemies who rise up against you to be defeated before you; they will come out against you one way and will flee before you seven ways.

"The LORD will command the blessing upon you in your barns and in all that you put your hand to, and He will bless you in the land which the LORD your God gives you.

"The LORD will establish you as a holy people to Himself, as He swore to you, if you keep the commandments of the LORD your God and walk in His ways.

"So all the peoples of the earth will see that you are called by the name of the LORD, and they will be afraid of you.

"The LORD will make you abound in prosperity, in the offspring of your body and in the offspring of your beast and in the produce of your ground, in the land which the LORD swore to your fathers to give you.

"The LORD will open for you His good storehouse, the heavens, to give rain to your land in its season and to bless all the work of your hand; and you shall lend to many nations, but you shall not borrow."

Reference Page

Chapter One

(1) *Holman's Old Testament Commentary*, Nashville, Tennessee: B&H Publishing Group, 2004, page 315.

(2) Charles Dickens *A Tale of Two Cities*, page 1, Everyman's Library, 1906, copyright by Simon Schama, published by Alfred A. Kropf, a division of Random House, Inc., New York, Everyman's Library, Northburgh House, London 1990.

Chapter Two

(3) Ruth Beechick, *Genesis, Finding Our Roots*, 1997 by Arrow Press, page 51.

Chapter Three

(4) *Footprints in the Sand*, Mary Stevenson, Permission granted by Basil Zangare, Copyright Owner, June 6, 2014.

Chapter Five

(5) Kubler-Ross MD, Elizabeth, *On Death and Dying*, New York: Routledge, 1973.

(6) Keller, Dixie Johnson Fraley, *The Widow's Workbook*, pages 45, 54, Aylen Publishing, 2003.

(7) Laura Story, *Blessings*, Capitol CMG Publishing, license 556247, EMI Christian Music Group, EMICMGMUSIC.

Chapter Eight

(8) Don and Sally Meredith, *Two Becoming One* www. book and workbook, www.2Becoming1.com.

Chapter Nine

(9) Kenneth Boa, Bruce Wilkinson, *Talk Through the Bible*, Nelson Publishers, page 67.

Chapter Ten

(10) Nicole Nordeman, *Love Story*, Worthy Publishing, 2012, page 191.

Appendix

(11) Permission was granted to use some concepts in the Blessing chapter from *The Father's Blessing* by William Ligon 4/4/14.

Recommended Reading List

Commentaries Researched in the writing of *Ruth: The Story Is In The Names*

The Bible Knowledge Commentary, Old Testament. By Walvord & Zuck. Victor Books, 198.

Bible Characters From the Old and New Testaments. Alexander Whyte. Kregel Publishers, 1896, 1999.

Matthew Henry's Commentary. Hendrickson Publishers, 1991.

Explore The Book. J. Sidlow Baxter. Zondervan Publishers, 1960.

Holman Old Testament Commentary on Judges, Ruth. by W. Gary Philllips. Holman Reference, 2004.

Books

Chapman, Mary Beth, *Choosing to SEE, A Journey of Struggle and Hope*, Revell, Grand Rapids, 2010

Crabb, Larry, *Shattered Dreams*. Colorado Springs: Waterbrook Press, 2001.

Barnhouse, Donald, *Invisible War*. Grand Rapids: Zondervan, 1965.

James, Carolyn Custis James, *The Gospel of Ruth*. Grand Rapids: Zondervan, 2008

Keller, Dixie Fraley, *The Widow's Workbook*. Aylen Publishing, Lake Mary, Florida. 2003.

Lewis, C.S. *A Grief Observed*. New York: Bantam, 1961.

Lewis, C.S. *The Problem of Pain*. New York: Simon and Schuster, 1996.

Neu, Sherry Boyd, *Rainbows After The Storm,* Sherry Boyd Neu, 2006

Sittser, Gerald, *A Grace Disguised: How the Soul Grows through Loss*. Grand Rapids: Zondervan, 2004

Vanauken, Sheldon. *A Severe Mercy*. New York: Harper and Row, 1977.

Yancy, Philip. *Where is God When It Hurts?* Grand Rapids: Zondervan, 1977.

Zonnebelt-Smeenge, R.N., Ed.D, DeVries, Robert C., D.Min., Ph.D., *Getting to the Other Side of Grief, Overcoming the Loss of a Spouse*. Baker Books, 1998.